NOV   2007

Ex-Etiquette

for

Holidays

and Other Family Celebrations

Jann Blackstone-Ford and Sharyl Jupe

CHICAGO
REVIEW
PRESS

D1413488

Library of Congress Cataloging-in-Publication Data
Blackstone-Ford, Jann.
    Ex-etiquette for holidays and other family celebrations / Jann Blackstone-
Ford and Sharyl Jupe. —1st ed.
        p. cm.
    Includes index.
    ISBN-13: 978-1-55652-719-7
    ISBN-10: 1-55652-719-5
    1. Stepfamilies. 2. Etiquette. 3. Remarried people—Family relationships.
4. Children of divorced parents—Family relationships. I.
    Jupe, Sharyl. II. Title.
    HQ759.92.B543 2008
    394.26—dc22
                                        2007018742

If you would like to ask the authors a question or schedule a workshop, you can
contact them through the Bonus Families Web site at www.bonusfamilies.com.

Cover and interior design: Rattray Design
Cover photo: Gabor Izso, © istockphoto.com
Author photo: Larry Ford

© 2008 by Jann Blackstone-Ford, M.A.
All rights reserved
First edition
Published by Chicago Review Press, Incorporated
814 North Franklin Street
Chicago, Illinois 60610
ISBN-13: 978-1-55652-719-7
ISBN-10: 1-55652-719-5
Printed in the United States of America
5 4 3 2 1

Contents

Acknowledgments

We would like to thank our collective family and friends for their understanding of the time it took us to write this book. Thanks to Larry, Melanie, Anee, Steven, and especially Harleigh for your support but most of all for being cheerleaders when we needed it.

Thank you to all the visitors to the Bonus Families Web site for your questions and suggestions and for your enthusiasm for our message. You are why we keep going. And your generous donations are *how* we keep going—thank you! Thanks to everyone at Chicago Review Press for your support and clear vision of why these books are needed, and thanks to Djana Pearson Morris, our literary agent, for her insight into the importance of finding a publisher like Chicago Review Press that is supportive of our work.

Finally, thanks to the one who said, "Blessed are the peacemakers" in times of conflict. You are our inspiration.

Introduction

Marrying Sharyl's ex-husband wasn't my idea—it was her daughter's. Melanie was only eight years old, and after months of sitting in a car while her father drove an hour and a half each way to see me, she just got tired of the drive. "Janny," she said from the backseat, "why don't you just move in with us? I hate driving back and forth."

"Funny you should say that," I remember saying, "Daddy and I were just talking about that this morning." And we were; we just didn't know how to break it to the kids. We also didn't know how to break it to Larry's ex-wife, Sharyl. That was only one of our dilemmas. In a couple of weeks it would be my husband's son's fourth birthday. Once I moved in, and we were officially a couple, we wondered, should we throw a party for little Steven and invite his mother? Or would she allow me to attend the party she was throwing for him? Or if Sharyl really went through the roof when she found out that we were moving in together (and planning to eventually marry), should we just plan on having two parties? We found ourselves analyzing every possible scenario and trying to choose the one that would result in the least amount of fallout.

The truth is, when you have children, especially if you and your ex share custody, the divorce itself is only the beginning of the issues to be hashed out. Life *after* divorce is what gets really confusing. And it's not just the big questions that set divorced parents on edge. It's the everyday questions, such as the ones we were facing, that divorced parents and their extended families find so perplexing. Should I invite my ex's new partner to my child's birthday party? Or where do we all sit at my child's soccer games?

The average couple today has a 43 percent chance of getting a divorce. In addition, over one-third of all babies born in the United States are born to single parents. Put these statistics together, and you realize that fewer children than ever before live in a conventional two-parent family, and there is a good chance that today's parents will raise their children with the help of someone other than their kids' biological mother or father. Add to that an increase in shared custody arrangements, and it's clear that children of divorce today continue to interact with both parents, the parents' new partners, extended family, and family friends long after their parents' divorce. As a result, former couples have to interact with each other to a greater extent than they did in years past. The rules that divorced parents used to live by no longer apply. We need new rules.

So what needs to change? First and foremost, divorced parents need to get better organized. They need to have a clear idea of how they will co-parent, how they will integrate new partners, and how their extended families will interact with their child, their child's other parent, and their child's other parent's extended family. That brings us to the reason for this book and the ex-etiquette books that came before it. In them you will find a guide for behavior that matches today's blended family lifestyle.

Sharyl, Larry, and I often say that if someone had sat down with us when we were in the midst of all our disagreements and simply said, "Stop that. Do you know what it is doing to the kids? Why don't you start looking for solutions instead of digging your heels in deeper?" we would have ended our war much sooner. We didn't know there was another way. We took it for granted that exes hate each other and fight over the kids. Over the years, we've found that everyone facing divorce or separation and then trying to start over has had the same hurdles to jump—and there wasn't much help out there. That's why, in 2000, using "cooperation and compromise" as our mantra and "the children" as our motivation, Sharyl and I started Bonus Families (www.bonusfamilies.com) as an online forum where divorced parents could get help with co-parenting issues. Now a non-profit organization, Bonus Families is the most visited divorce and stepfamily site on the Web. Bonus Families offers counseling, mediation, support, and education to anyone who has to deal with a divorce or separation, not just those who have children.

Motivated by the tremendous response to Bonus Families, Sharyl and I started writing these books. In our first book, *Ex-Etiquette for Parents*, we established the "Ten Rules of Good Ex-Etiquette" and applied them to co-parenting after divorce or separation. Our second book, *Ex-Etiquette for Weddings*, similarly established ten rules of good ex-etiquette for encore weddings and weddings of adult children of divorce. In this book you will find ten rules of good ex-etiquette for holidays and other family celebrations (see page 3), along with lots of examples of the rules' practical applications. The rules of good ex-etiquette always start with "Put the children first." If you don't have children, then the key to getting along after a divorce or separation is simply to follow the golden rule, "Treat others as you would like to be treated."

We believe that good behavior begins with your mental attitude. For that reason we begin each ex-etiquette book with a chapter on laying the groundwork. By that we mean checking your attitude and getting your thoughts in order before interacting with an ex, former in-laws, an ex's new partner, or your divorced parents. If you haven't laid the proper groundwork, then spite, jealousy, or revenge rear up with a vengeance, and positive communication becomes impossible. So in this book we will help you lay the mental groundwork first, and then apply what you have learned to the situations you face.

We know that everyone responds to divorce differently and that some breakups are fresher or far more traumatic than others. With this in mind, there are times when we address a conflict by using what we call the "1-2-3 approach," in which various problem-solving approaches are suggested depending on your level of comfort when interacting with your ex. For example, let's say you want to make a change in your child's visitation schedule for Christmas. Using the "1-2-3 approach," a level 1 action might be to send an e-mail to your ex. You are so angry or hurt you don't want to talk in person, but you have to communicate somehow, so you initiate a *polite* e-mail. Although it is not the optimal method of communication, it is—by far—more appropriate than sending information through your child (something that is *not* good ex-etiquette, and we do our best to call that to the attention of divorced parents at every possible opportunity). A level 2 approach might be a polite phone call. (Note that word *polite* again. My grandmother used to repeat, "You can catch more flies with honey than with vinegar.") You are still uncomfortable interacting face-to-face, but you can now handle the sound of each other's voice. If you've reached level 3, then cordial face-to-face interaction is comfortable and commonplace. Both divorced parents have released their animosity and can make decisions based on the best interests of the kids. If you are interacting at level 3, then you have reached *bonus* status—the ultimate goal—and that is what using good ex-etiquette is all about. It is important to note that level 3 does not imply that you, your ex, and his or her new partner are necessarily all pals who go shopping and play golf together! It simply means that interaction is comfortable, and all decisions are based on *putting the kids first* (if there are children to be considered).

As you read this book you will notice that sometimes we use various words as catchalls. For example, we know that some couples or parents never marry, or that some are separated and not yet divorced, but it's difficult to capture every state of every relationship, so when talking about a breakup, most of the time we use the word *divorce*. We also refer to "old-school divorce philosophy" as opposed to "new-school divorce philosophy." The former refers to the expectation of interaction after divorce that has prevailed for years, which is that people who have broken up no longer talk to each other—and they certainly don't cooperate with each other. The new-school philosophy refers to the approach we advocate today: positive interaction between divorced individuals, with the desire to problem-solve when and as necessary.

You may also notice that we usually use the word *bonus* in lieu of *step-*. We began using the word in our early days as a combined family as a more positive way to refer to the "step" experience. Personally, I didn't like being called a stepmother. It brought to mind a wicked woman who resented the kids in her care, when that couldn't have been further from the truth. To reinforce my discomfort with the word, one day my "stepdaughter," Melanie, confided that she did not like to introduce me as her stepmother because then her friends automatically thought that she didn't like me. Thank goodness Sharyl's main concern was her daughter's comfort level. It enabled us to put our heads together and come up with another word to better describe the "step" relationship—and the word we chose was *bonus*. A bonus is a reward for a job well done. And my husband's children were definitely a bonus in my life. Plus, *bonus* transforms quite well into bonusmom rather than stepmom and bonusdad rather than stepdad. Blended mom and blended dad just don't have the same ring. So throughout this book we often use the words *bonus*, *blended*, and *step* interchangeably.

We also use the term *counterpartner* to describe the relationship between a mom and a bonusmom or a dad and a bonusdad. Custody arrangements today often involve bonusparents performing some of the same duties as biological parents. I know I am not Sharyl's children's mother, but I have been called upon to perform some of the same duties as Sharyl in regard to their care. Getting along with an ex starts with the proper mind-set, and the same holds true for dealing with your spouse's ex or your ex's new partner. Sharyl and I recognize that we are partners of a sort in raising the kids; hence, we came up with the term *counterpartner*.

Finally, you may notice that the voice in which this book is written is mine, Jann's voice. That's because it is very difficult for two people to write a book together, each in her own voice. We tried it, and it didn't work. So we opted to use one voice. That voice ended up being mine, but you can be assured that Sharyl has contributed to and reviewed every aspect of the writing of this book.

We would love to hear from you. If you would like to contact us to ask a question or book a bonusparenting workshop, please feel free to e-mail us via the Bonus Families Web site.

1

Laying the Groundwork for Family Gatherings

"The true test of intelligence is not how much we know how to do, but how we behave when we don't know what to do."

—John Holt, author and educator

Your behavior in a time of stress and conflict determines whether the conflict will accelerate or will serve as an opportunity to problem-solve. Over the years, Sharyl and I have

1

found that facing a conflict isn't necessarily a bad thing. Conflict can be a way to call attention to something that needs to be changed—to recognize a difference of opinion, discuss the differences, and find a solution—and we apply this attitude to just about every interaction with our exes—or each other for that matter.

Many of us were raised with the old-school philosophy that interaction with an ex ends with the breakup. Why would anyone want to interact with an ex? After all, he or she is part of the past. Time to move on, right? For some people that may be true, but for those who share children, or perhaps a business, friends, relatives, even pets, after a breakup, dealing with an ex can be very much in the present. The boundaries associated with dealing with an ex today are blurry at best. As a result, a completely new type of communication must be learned that enables exes to easily interact. We call it good ex-etiquette.

What Is Ex-Etiquette?

Years ago Emily Post explained that etiquette is "a code of behavior based on consideration, kindness, and unselfishness." *Ex*-etiquette is simply applying that code to interaction with your ex. Many people will laugh at the prospect of interacting politely with an ex. Most exes go out of their way *not* to be around each other. If they do happen to end up under the same roof, one might head for the door or possibly hole up in the bathroom until the other has gone. But given our changing, more relaxed social mores, the increase in joint custody arrangements, and the trend toward more involved co-parenting, families need a new set of guidelines to follow. If divorced couples (and their extended families) want to peacefully share in the major milestones of their children's lives, or if they want to combine families in such a way that the kids don't experience divided loyalties, they can look to the rules of good ex-etiquette for guidance.

The Ten Rules of Good Ex-Etiquette for Holidays and Other Family Celebrations

No one can get your blood boiling quite as quickly as a former spouse. Unfortunately, when you are in that state it makes it impossible to make good decisions for your children. Bonus Families is often asked for some quick tips to which parents can refer—something they can remember at the peak of their anger that will bring them back to what is important—their children's welfare. That's why we developed the "Ten Rules of Good Ex-Etiquette" years ago. We have adapted the original rules to apply expressly to holidays and family get-togethers. If you remember only one thing when attempting to resolve a conflict with an ex or former family member, the first rule, "Put the children first," will always steer you in the right direction.

The Ten Rules of Good Ex-Etiquette for Holidays and Other Family Celebrations

1. Put the children first.
2. Remember the spirit of the special occasion or holiday.
3. Never badmouth your ex, extended-family members, the host, or others.
4. Get organized well in advance.
5. Don't be spiteful.
6. Don't hold grudges.
7. Use empathy when problem solving.
8. Be honest and straightforward.
9. Respect each other's turf, holiday rituals, and family traditions.
10. Compromise whenever possible.

A New Way of Thinking

Sharyl and I understand how easily an ex can push your buttons—we have both experienced emotionally charged breakups. The memories associated with a breakup are rarely positive, and it's important to understand how those memories can affect your present attitude and behavior to the point that even the smallest interaction with your ex becomes intolerable.

Let's say that hiking over the rocks at the seashore is one of your favorite activities. It's something you have done for many years to relax and get some exercise. There's one place near your home that you particularly like. It's steep and dangerous but lovely at the same time, and you love the way the salt smells in the air and how the colors change as the sun sets over the rocks. The last time you ventured out on your hike, however, you slipped and fell. Your arm was broken, and the pain was excruciating. No one was around to help, and you had to drive to the nearest hospital by yourself. As you drove, you mentally rehashed the fall. You examined your arm about twenty times, and each time you saw yourself falling in your mind. You got to the hospital, and the doctor told you that an operation would be needed to set the bone properly. There would be a scar, and since your arm was broken in a few places the healing process would be long, painful, and difficult.

Later, once your arm has healed, do you think you will be anxious to go back to your favorite place? The sea still smells the same. The way the sun hits the rocks at sunset hasn't changed. But the way you think about your favorite place has shifted, because now you associate climbing on those rocks not with comfort but with pain. And each time you look at your arm and see the scar, it reminds you of the pain you had to endure.

We hope that the metaphor is obvious. At one point many of us found comfort with other partners, only to be faced later with a painful breakup. Now we no longer associate our former partners with anything positive, only with anger and pain. We remember what they did to us—or what we did to them—and hurt prevents us from positive interactions. We anticipate seeing them again and immediately start feeling the anger, resentment, regret, embarrassment, or guilt associated with those previous interactions. Our preconceived notions color our attitude about interaction, and when we are invited to a special occasion along with someone who conjures up these awful feelings, we either do not want to go or resent that we have to, which only perpetuates the negative thoughts–negative behavior chain of events. What to do?

Break Old Thought Patterns

It's hard work to interact with someone who may have hurt you—especially if he or she is now happy and you're not, which just adds insult to injury—and it's understandable if you have resigned yourself to being a "justified-for-being-angry" victim. But if you can change your thoughts about and negative associations of your ex, you can change your behavior toward him or her when you have to interact. Eventually, you will no longer feel like a victim or dread interacting with your ex.

Why is positive interaction with your ex so important? First, if you have children, you're not just interacting with your ex but with your children's father or mother. Granted, your ex may have been a jerk to you, but this has nothing to do with his or her parental responsibility and ability. You *will* have to interact with your child's other parent now and forever. The quicker you can rise above your ex's poor behavior, the better parent *you* will be. You will be able to enjoy your child's milestone events and family celebrations. Finally, you will be free of the past and feel like you are in positive control of your life and your family.

Here's a personal story that illustrates how to break the old negative thoughts–negative behavior chain. Larry and I had been married for six months, and during that time Sharyl and I were constantly at odds. We never had any issues of jealousy over my husband—her ex. For us it was always issues with the kids. We suffered from what I call the "Best Family Syndrome." Each of us feared that the kids would prefer to be at the other's home, with the "best family." This fear put us in a state of constant conflict—Sharyl and I were always angry about something. In addition, although I never would have admitted it then, now I can easily say that I resented the kids' having to go back and forth between homes every other week, and I worried about how it affected all of them—Larry and Sharyl's two, my daughter from a previous marriage, and later, when Larry and I had a daughter, the little one as well.

This particular time it was the kids' spring break. Even though there was a set visitation schedule, spring break was not part of the holidays' split, so whoever had the kids that week automatically had them for the entire vacation. The kids' father and I wanted to stick to the visitation schedule, because we had them through the break and wanted to take them on some special day trips. I just knew Sharyl would want to change things in some way. As spring break got closer, I began to get anxious.

Preparing dinner each night was a time when I was alone. I'd stop working at about four o'clock in the afternoon. The kids were doing homework, their dad wasn't home yet, and there was no one around to distract me. As I took out all the utensils to begin the preparations I'd start hashing things over in my mind. Life was pretty stressful in those days, and Sharyl and I were each always convinced that the other had an ulterior motive, some kind of strategy to win the kids' time and affection.

As I'd begin to prepare dinner each night I'd think, "I know exactly what she is going to do. She's going to try to take the kids to

Disneyland during the break." As I chopped up vegetables I'd think something like, "And she's going to call us up and ask if she could have the kids for an extended weekend so she can do that." As I sautéed the vegetables I'd think, "We can't afford Disneyland, and then *my daughter* will be sad because she can't go." With each step of the preparation I'd layer on a new worry: how do I explain to her that Melanie and Steven can go to Disneyland but she can't? I did this day after day until I found myself dreading to walk into the kitchen to cook dinner. And I like to cook! What was going on?

That's when I took a hard look at my thought process while preparing the food. With each step of the preparation I became angrier until all my joy was gone. I subconsciously connected preparing dinner with my angry thoughts—so I avoided preparing dinner.

This was a huge revelation to me. I realized at that moment that if I had thought myself into being angry, I could think myself out of it. I made a vow to change what I thought about as I prepared dinner. Instead of anticipating something negative, I concentrated on my love for my family—in this case how much I enjoyed preparing a meal. I began to mentally liken each step of the preparation to wrapping a present for my loved ones. First, I took note of how happy I was to be married to my husband. He loves to eat, and I envisioned his smile when he realized I was making his favorite dinner. Next, rather than worry that my daughter would be slighted by a decision Sharyl might make, I took note of the privilege I felt to be included as a caregiver to her wonderful kids. I thought about how happy I was that they had fully accepted my daughter as their sister. And, I had to admit, those wonderful kids were half Sharyl's, and rather than resent her I needed to respect her for being their mother.

Over the next few days, not only did I reclaim my enjoyment of preparing dinner for my family but also, because of my new attitude, the next time I talked to Sharyl I didn't have one bad thing to say to her. Oh, and one more thing: she never did request extra time to take the kids to Disneyland!

Changing your thoughts about someone will change not only your own mood but also the way you approach the other person at your next meeting. You cannot control someone else's thoughts, but you certainly can have control of your own. When you control your thoughts, you control your life; you break the negative thoughts–negative behavior chain, and everyone wins.

The Importance of Tact and Timing

Tact and timing are two major components in preventing a communication breakdown with an ex or an ex's new partner. For example, if you are late picking up your child from your ex's house, and he or she has been waiting for an hour, it might not be a really good occasion to ask for extra time with the child next week! A better choice would be to wait a few days and then call. During your conversation, try, "Hey, I'm sorry I kept you waiting last time. I will be on time next time." After he or she accepts your apology, *then* say, "By the way, the Raiders are playing this weekend, and you know how much Zach loves the Raiders. I was thinking about getting tickets, but he'll be with you on Sunday. Is there any way to rearrange the schedule so that I can take him to the game?"

Or let's say you just happen to see your ex out and about. It's her turn to have the kids, and you wonder who the heck is watching them. Saying, "Having fun? So, who's is watching Kayla and Zachary?" may not be a good choice if you want to avoid a public argument. A more tactful approach would be to say, "Boy, it's difficult to find good babysitters. I have a heck of a time finding someone the kids like. Who did you call? . . . Maybe we should keep things consistent from house to house, and I will ask her to babysit when I need a sitter?" That's using good ex-etiquette *and* tact and timing in your interaction.

There will be times when exes have every right to ask questions, but be smart about when you ask. Before you speak, think. Because if you share something with your ex, whether it's kids, a business, an animal, or even friends, this will not be the last time you talk to this person—communication is ongoing.

Set the Example for Good Communication

People often complain, "But my ex won't cooperate with me. I can't make communication with my ex work all by myself." Yes, you can. Like most people, you probably believe that communication is a two-way street. If one of you puts up a barrier to cordial interaction, then it is unlikely things will change. But things *can* change if even one person is committed to positive interaction. Some call it the power of attraction. Some call it karma. Some would say you reap what you sow. We've already talked about developing a new mind-set when dealing with your ex—one that breaks the negative thoughts–negative behavior chain. So let's assume you now change your belief about your ex before you interact. Your attitude and behavior are now different, and you'll be amazed at how your positive example alone can make the outcome of your interaction different.

This is when people typically say something like "But I *have* changed my attitude toward my ex, and my ex still hasn't changed. How do I get him to return my phone calls?" The "How do I get x to do y?" question is one of the most common we receive. Basically, the person is asking, "How do I make someone do what *I* want them to do instead of what *they* want to do?" In other words, how can I control the outcome? The answer, of course, is that you can't control anyone. How your ex responds to you depends upon the groundwork you have laid. If you find that someone is difficult, it could be that they are negatively anticipating a meeting with *you*. They don't want to deal with you either! Know this: you can only control yourself—

your thoughts, your actions. You can lead by example. If you want your phone calls returned, make sure you return phone calls. If you don't like it when your ex is late, don't try to get even or to exact payback by being late yourself. I learned from personal experience that changing my thoughts and behavior toward Sharyl brought about a larger change in our relationship. Dwell on the positive and you will behave positively, and soon the other person will, too. It all begins with you.

Don't Play the Victim

In saying that *you* need to change *your* attitude and behavior, I don't mean to suggest that it's all your fault, that "it's all in your head," or to underestimate how miserable divorce can be, or to minimize the hurt and resentment that you may justifiably still feel. Divorce is one of the most painful experiences we can face. One of the reasons people cling to their anger, resentment, or even jealousy after a divorce is because they sense that once those emotions are gone, the only thing that will be left is the pain. Anger and jealousy can serve as Band-Aids for that pain. If your ex perceives you as angry and adjusts his or her behavior accordingly, then you have control—and that makes you right. To be right in the face of a breakup—that's the ultimate vindication. You're the good guy. It wasn't your fault, no matter what happened. Hold on to that anger and you will remain the wronged one and the good guy forever.

But you will also remain in a state of anger forever. And when you are angry you diminish your personal power. Why? Because when you are angry you are reacting to something that has happened *to* you. That means you aren't controlling your emotions or the outcome—they are controlling you. The ironic thing about being angry is that it's usually wasted energy. Rarely do the people you are angry with understand the depth of your emotion. Your anger has no effect on them, especially if they are not around to see you angry.

Here's a perfect example. The phone rings; you know it's your ex, and you start to think what a miserable person he or she is—she left you, he's not paying child support but still wants to see the kids, and on and on. By the time you've answered the phone you're so angry that you're ready to bite your ex's head off. Your ex in turn hears the tone of your voice or your attitude and thinks, "This person is such a ^%$#@. I haven't said a thing, and this ^%$#@ is already on my case." The stage has been set. No one will win. You can do your best to make someone else's life miserable, but to do that, you also have to stay in a miserable, victimized state.

Envision the Relationship You Want

Moving forward begins with developing a mental picture for the relationship you want to have with your ex. When you anticipate your next meeting, do you picture a calm interaction? Or do you picture yourself screaming at him or her for all the wrongs perpetrated against you? Do you see a calm encounter with former relatives, or do you envision everyone lining up on either side of the room throwing poisonous stares? In other words, what do *you* want? How do *you* envision interacting? Think about what it will take to achieve that positive interaction, and then do it. Don't picture *their* reaction, because it doesn't matter. Picture only what you want, what you expect, and the type of relationship you want to have, then put one foot in front of the other to get there. It may take more than one try, but it will work. Your life will be different, and you will not be dependent on the reaction of an ex, former relatives, or friends for your happiness.

Here's another take on these issues, but this time from an ex-in-law's point of view:

"My daughter got a divorce from a guy who had a drug problem. He's clean and sober now, but he put her through hell. They have two kids, so he's still in the picture. But I can barely be in the same room with him; how can I possibly get along with him?"

The rules for good ex-etiquette are not just for parents. They are for anyone who has to deal with divorce or separation. It is just as important for grandparents to remember "Put the children first" as it is for parents. The principle here really isn't any different for you than it is for someone dealing with an uncooperative ex. Changing your thinking to control your behavior does not mean that you blindly accept your ex-son-in-law's past behavior. It is a way for you to release your resentment so that you can comfortably interact with him in spite of negative things that have happened in the past. It will help if you realize that improving your relationship starts with just one attempt at being cordial and then building on that. Don't get ahead of yourself: clearly you intensely dislike this guy, so imagining that you have to be nice to him for the rest of your life will likely be quite frustrating.

You might be thinking, "But he's hurt someone I love. And he's not a big part of *my* life anymore, so I can act any way I want the few times I do see him." That's really not true. We are role models for everyone around us, and the next time you see him will probably be at a family gathering where others—especially his children—are watching. If you set a positive example and produce a positive outcome, someone someday may be in a similar position and take a cue from how they saw you handle the situation. As a grandparent you have the opportunity to offer your grandchildren an example of forgiveness, tolerance, and compassion, but more important, the wisdom to know the difference. That's a wonderful legacy to pass on.

Putting Good Ex-Etiquette into Practice: Guidelines for Family Gatherings

Let's take everything we've discussed and look at how these concepts work in some practical applications, using as examples the types of real-life dilemmas divorced people face when trying to navigate family gatherings.

Introductions

Sharyl and I are often asked how to handle tricky introductions. Say you are at a family gathering and find yourself having to introduce a bonusrelative, an ex, or another ex-relative.

When making the introduction it's your job to make people feel comfortable. So think, "What do they have in common? What can I tell each person about the other so they will feel comfortable and have something to talk about once I leave?" And, just as important, "What would they like me *not* to say for now?" It's not necessary to volunteer everything you know about someone during a first introduction, especially if there is a long and winding marital history.

> *"I am a married woman with two children. What would be the correct way to introduce the woman my father married after my mother's death? Should I introduce her as my stepmother?"*

Technically, she is your stepmother, or bonusmom if you have become close, but it is understandable if you feel uncomfortable referring to her as such. Children who grow up thinking of the person as a parent figure or special friend more often use such terms. It can be more awkward to refer to someone as a stepparent or bonusparent if you've met them for the first time as an adult—and they may not feel comfortable with the description either. So in this case it is perfectly appropriate to refer to her as "my father's wife."

"How do I introduce my ex-wife's parents? I'm remarried but am still close to them. Do I call them my ex-in-laws?"

Many divorced people remain close to their ex-husband's or ex-wife's family even though they have remarried. This is particularly the case when the divorced couple has children. Then your ex-relations are your child's grandma or grandpa, aunts or uncles, and you should perpetuate these relationships in the best interests of the child. The same is true if one person in a marriage dies. The surviving spouse often stays close to the deceased's parents, first because of a bond built during the marriage but also because of the necessity to support their children's relationship with their deceased spouse's extended family.

So, using the children as common ground, you would introduce former in-laws as your child's grandparents: "May I introduce Mary Miller, my son's grandmother?" If you have no children, but still remain close to former in-laws, you might want to ask yourself whether it is even necessary to explain that they are your ex's parents. You may want to say "dear friend" or "like a mother or father" during the introduction. If you feel it is important to mention their former status, perhaps out of respect for a deceased husband or wife, then you should refer to them as the parents of your former or deceased spouse, not your ex. *Ex* implies divorce.

"My ex-husband's daughter and I remain close. Is she considered my ex-stepdaughter or my stepdaughter? How do I introduce her? Also, since she is now grown and has a daughter, do I introduce her daughter as my granddaughter, my step-grand-daughter, or something else?"

Names and titles can get quite confusing when there has been more than one marriage. Theoretically, you can preface any past relationship with the prefix "ex." It means former. Although it is most often used in regard to divorced husbands and wives, it can also be used to describe other relationships. A former boss, for example, would be your *ex-boss* or your *ex-employer*. If your ex-husband had a daughter from a previous marriage, and you are now divorced, his daughter could be called your "ex-stepdaughter" if you like.

Personally, I never liked being called a stepmom, nor did I like calling my husband's children my stepkids. That's why we came up with the term *bonus*. The kids were definitely a bonus to my life when I married their dad, and they still would be even if Larry and I split up. The "bonus" status does not change when you divorce. So if you are searching for a label for your ex-husband's daughter that describes your relationship to each other but is not dependent on your relationship with her father, try "bonusdaughter," because that can describe your past, present, and future relationship. Following the same logic, her daughter would then be called your bonusgranddaughter.

If you do not feel comfortable with the *bonus* title, then introducing her as "my dear (or good or special) friend whom I love like a daughter" is also appropriate.

Family Transition Time After Divorce

Divorced families often have a difficult time during that period of transition right after the divorce, when a family moves from doing things as a two-parent family to mom and dad doing things separately with the kids.

The family below is trying to take a contemporary approach after divorce; but without clear boundaries it's easy to frustrate and confuse family members.

"My ex-wife and I parted on equitable terms two years ago. Although she has primary placement of our two boys, I see the

kids a couple times a week, and we try to all have dinner together at least once a week to ease the kids into our no longer living together. Most of the time we play a board game or something and call it 'game night.' My new wife is uncomfortable with this practice continuing. My kids, however, enjoy the time spent with both parents each week. I am a devoted husband and dad and have tried to change game night to just 'Dad's night with the kids,' but my ex and kids are resentful. Help!"

The parent-child relationship should, of course, be perpetuated after divorce or separation, but not the husband-wife relationship—at least not on the same level as it was when you were married. Game night is great in theory, but in reality, unless the parents have spent some time apart and have set a precedent for being apart, continuing to interact as a family immediately after divorce is just plain confusing for kids. It could extend their period of adjustment after the divorce and make it difficult for them to connect with another adult when Mom or Dad meets someone new. Remember that kids, no matter their age, often harbor a desire for their mom and dad to reconcile. If they see that their amicably divorced mom and dad are no longer speaking because one of them has a new partner, the chances that the kids will have a positive relationship with that new partner will be next to nothing. Something like game night is best experienced after time apart—as part of an evolution to a cordial relationship between divorced parents for the sake of the kids, not as an excuse to wean the kids from family life. (In truth, this approach is sometimes a way to wean the *parents*, not the kids, from their old life. If that is the case, maybe reconciliation *should* be considered.)

So what are the proper boundaries? The best answer is that if the family get-together involves the kids—Christmas, birthdays, graduations—then that is a time when cordial interaction between parent figures and kids is possible. Other holidays or celebrations that don't involve kids need not be spent together. Dad's promotion or "taco Tuesday" at your house? That's new-family time, when you should be establishing your own new memories.

It's important to establish clear boundaries early. As time goes on, new people will come into your life, and it will be easier for everyone if clear boundaries are already in place and all the players know up front what is expected of them. At this point, however, a little later in the game, you may have to have a conversation with your ex to clarify your priorities. You might want to mention that, of all people, your ex should understand that your *adult-relationship priorities* must lie with your new spouse—but that this fact will in no way impede your ability to remain active in your children's lives.

When You Would Rather Not Attend a Family Gathering

There will be times when you feel that your situation with your ex is so complicated that you simply do not want to attend a family gathering. Before you opt out, however, think twice. You may be hurting loved ones and sending the wrong message.

> *"My sister-in-law insists on inviting my husband's ex-girlfriend (and the mother of his son) to every family gathering. I have tried to get along with her, but she is a very unpleasant person. I don't think I will attend my sister-in-law's parties anymore. Am I wrong?"*

In a word, yes. You're probably going to these parties in the first place to support your husband and be part of the family. The way you feel about the mother of your husband's child has nothing to do with the reason you attend. By *not* going you're basically saying, "I care more about this person who gets on my nerves than the person whom I love." That's not the message you want to send.

People who marry someone with children must be primed. Those children have *two* parents—your spouse and someone else—and it's very likely that at some point you will all appear at family gatherings together. Granted, the fact that your husband's ex, whom you dislike, is so entwined in his family's affairs can be aggravating, but it need not drive you away. By going to these parties you are putting down roots and establishing your own place. If you stop going, it will most likely cause resentment and talk among family members and make it less likely that you will be regarded as part of the family.

Although you may not see it, your sister-in-law is between a rock and a hard place. Just like a divorced couple facing the aftermath of breakup, she, too, is juggling past and present people in her life. Even though your husband never married the mother of his child, his ex is still his sister's nephew's mother—maybe even a close friend. She's doing exactly what I suggest: invite everyone to the party and let them choose to either attend or decline. The only prerequisite is that they act like adults for the sake of the children looking on.

All of us have friends and family whom we don't care for, and breakups and remarriage have a tendency to add people to the list. The key to coping is to use the rules of good ex-etiquette as your guide—the primary rule of which is "Put the children first." This means you don't allow yourself to get caught up in melodrama; you look for your higher self, and you go to the parties right alongside your husband.

Uninvited Guests

Another way to put good ex-etiquette into practice at family gatherings is to know when in fact you should *not* attend a gathering, as the scenario below illustrates.

"My children overheard my ex-husband's new wife say that I
was 'tacky' for attending my ex-in-laws' family functions!

Technically, I do not receive a direct invitation, but because my kids were there, and neither my former in-laws nor my ex-husband have ever asked me to leave, I assume that I am welcome. Is my assumption tacky, or is my ex-husband's new wife just jealous and threatened by my presence?"

Your assumption that you are invited to family get-togethers at your former in-laws' home *is* tacky. I don't know if your ex's new wife is threatened or not, but I do know that it's also tacky for her to say something in front of your children. Talking behind your back with children present is very poor ex-etiquette. If she has a problem, she should take it up with you and the hostess.

You remain the children's mother after a divorce, of course, but you do not remain your ex's partner. This new couple needs time to bond not only emotionally but also in the eyes of other family members. Because of this, there may be times when the new partner should attend social affairs while you should not. The ultimate goal is for everyone to be comfortable when you see one another. If this is achieved, you will probably be included on the guest list for special occasions but not for every family get-together. You should always wait for an invitation.

There is a reason you have not been invited by the hostess; don't assume that you should be there just because you haven't been asked to leave. Good ex-etiquette states that if you are invited to special occasion get-togethers, consider it a great compliment and go. But for everyday family get-togethers, give your ex, his new wife, and their extended family their space.

2

Ex-Etiquette for Holidays

"We are divorced, we are friends, and we are good parents."
—Sarah Ferguson (formerly married to
Prince Andrew, Duke of York)

The concept of *family* seems to be synonymous with holidays, whether it's Christmas, Hanukkah, or even Valentine's Day. Most holidays serve as a reason to come together, count our blessings, and acknowledge family and friendship. But if you or someone in your family has faced divorce, holidays may not always feel like a cause for celebration. Just the logistics of deciding where to hold the holiday festivities after a couple breaks up can be trying. Should we meet at Mom's house? Dad's house? Grandma and Grandpa's house? Some wonder whether they should celebrate in the same manner as before the divorce, whereas others are concerned that their cherished family traditions will be lost altogether. It is possible to turn a holiday into a relaxed, happy occasion, but it takes time and hard work to pull yourself up by the bootstraps when you are feeling overwhelmed.

Have Reasonable Expectations

Many people have grown up with an *It's a Wonderful Life* sort of TV-infused expectation of a merry Christmas, but few of us really experience that sort of holiday, especially if family members are going every which way trying to spend time with "your relatives," "my relatives," and "former relatives" all in one day. As a result, it's not uncommon for the stress of coordinating the holidays to make divorced parents want to just stop celebrating. The kids do their best to cope—after all, many get double or even triple presents—but parents find themselves overcompensating to make sure the kids receive something at every home, from both sides of the family. Many parents comment that the spirit of the holiday is simply lost once divorced.

Having reasonable expectations for the holidays is the first step toward bringing the holiday spirit back after your divorce and making them run more smoothly. This means, look at your life as it is right now; don't try to re-create the way things used to be before the divorce, because they simply won't be the same. For some people this is a good thing, because the tension in the marriage before the divorce made the holidays unbearable. So they look to a brighter future. Others mourn the passing of "family time" and want their old life back. But holding on to the past—whether you view the past as positive or negative—is simply setting yourself up for failure.

This is when many people ask, "Well, isn't that what you are sup-posed to do? Try to do everything as you always did? Won't it hurt less?" And if they have children, they add, "so the kids don't feel the sting of the divorce." Not really. Everyone, no matter what age, knows that divorce changes things. Just because your children might be very young and cannot communicate exactly how they feel does not mean they can't sense a change in their life. Of course parents should do their best to "keep a stiff upper lip" so that the kids feel safe and secure, but to totally deny a change—to act like nothing has happened—can interfere with everyone's healing process and extend their period of adjustment.

The only thing about holidays of which divorced people can be certain is that things will not be the same as when they were married. Try not to compare before and after. Make an effort to change the way you do things now. Do anything and everything you can to be proactive and put a new, positive spin on your holiday.

Helping Your Child Transition from House to House

Holidays become stressful for children when they see that their par-ents (both bonus and biological) are vindictive, floundering, and dis-organized. Being organized will ensure that the kids feel safe and secure, willing to accept the inevitable changes between past and present.

There are some changes divorced parents can make that will help ease their children's transition from house to house during the holi-days. Note that I didn't say "suggestions for parents to cope with the holidays." If you are practicing good ex-etiquette, your goal is to cre-ate an environment where your children can flourish; therefore, you have to make the necessary changes. Your ability to cope is a result of the positive changes you make.

Begin by making the transition from house to house as stress-free as you can by coordinating efforts with your child's other parent well in advance. Knowing exactly what time your child will leave (or when you will pick the child up) and planning for it—bags packed at the door rather than scrambling around at the last minute—will help.

When your child leaves, avoid saying things like "I'm going to miss you so much." Even if you are, saying so just makes the transition more difficult for the child. Give a hug and a few loving words, and then let the child go. Agree on a time you will check in, and stick to it. Do not call every five minutes to check up or to repeat that he or she is the most important thing in your life. This is quite disruptive for the other home and actually causes kids more anxiety than comfort. Parents whose children are truly the most important thing in their lives allow them to settle in at the other parent's home so they can enjoy their time together. Constantly calling with reminders that you miss your child is not putting your child first—it's putting your child in the middle.

It also helps to coordinate presents with your kids' other parent. Decide who is going to give Jordan the bike and Jenna the Rollerblades. Follow the rules of good ex-etiquette and look for the compromise. Then let everything go. Don't stew over the agreement you just made: "I should have said this" or "I should have held out for more time." Move on and celebrate the day. Be the example.

Handling Family Traditions

Family traditions and rituals are what give us that feeling of family. And part of what is special about family traditions is who participates in them. If the players change—say everyone always assembles at Grandma and Grandpa's house on Christmas Day, but then they divorce or one of them passes away—there is a feeling that the tradition has been broken.

One of the most poignant letters I have ever received was from a young man returning home from college during Christmas vacation. His family had always congregated at his aunt and uncle's for the holidays, but they had divorced six months earlier. Although he loved his immediate family dearly, the fact that his favorite aunt and uncle were no longer hosting Christmas at their home really upset him. He was writing to ask how to help his family members handle the change. He inherently understood that divorce affects everyone in the family, not just the couple divorcing.

If there has been a breakup, the key is to try to modify the past tradition, not abandon it. You save the traditions you love, and you alter the ones that no longer work. Look for ways to keep parts of the family tradition but add new aspects that will raise everyone's spirits and get their mind off "the way it used to be" or "the way it *should* be." Little things help. Buy a new holiday CD instead of the one you always used to play. Add a few new decorations around the house. Invite friends over instead of just being alone. Cook a new meal, or buy takeout! Do something just a little bit different that acknowledges both the past and the present—and then put one foot in front of the other.

Let's look at how you can modify a family ritual or custom so that you can honor the past but look forward to the future. In the young man's case, he might prompt his parents or another family member to host Christmas Day at their home, but to include some of the same family traditions formerly observed at the aunt and uncle's home. They can alter the traditions by learning to associate the family customs with the holidays, not necessarily with the aunt and uncle as a couple. For example, a holiday tradition at our home is that we make caramel apples for dessert. The kids love to dip the apples in the caramel, decorate the apples, and trade them with a family member—and they can do this at any family member's home. Since we trade off who hosts the holidays each year, the tradition is now the making of caramel apples, not necessarily that the holiday celebration is held at my house or at Sharyl's house. The trick is to acknowledge the change but not abandon the family tradition.

It may be time to modify a family tradition again when someone remarries. A well-adjusted bonusfamily attempts to combine both families' rituals to create new family rituals that work for them. They cherish the similarities and respect the differences. And, if need be, they start from scratch and establish new traditions of their own.

I remember how one year around the holidays I realized that my family had no holiday traditions. I was feeling sorry for myself, thinking we had tried hard to do everything right, yet Christmas was rolling around and my family—now that we were "blended"—had no family Christmas identity. I called Sharyl to enlist her help to coordinate something the kids could look forward to. Sharyl talked about the things she liked about Christmas at her house—how when they decorated the tree they discussed each ornament. "Remember when we got this ornament?" "Remember when we did that?" And how they all laughed at the stories they told. I realized we did something very similar at our home, and it was one of the things I loved about decorating for the holidays, but I hadn't regarded it as a "tradition." It started me thinking about what a family tradition really is and how we can make the holidays happy by calling attention to what comes naturally—like talking about ornaments or making caramel apples. *We* make our holidays happy. We *did* have family traditions of our own. I just didn't see them.

Celebrating the Holidays with Your Ex

Whether or not you celebrate the holidays with your ex may depend on how long you have been divorced and the degree of tension between you. Most former couples are angry and resentful right after they suffer a breakup, and if you are still facing those kinds of emotions, enlisting family and friends to sit around the fire sipping eggnog is asking too much of them.

If you have children and they want to try it, celebrating with your ex may be something to consider after enough time has passed and emotions are not so high. But don't push it on anyone. Some children actually feel uncomfortable when their divorced parents are too friendly—afraid that the other shoe may drop at any minute. So follow your kids' lead on this one. If your family is not ready to interact on this level after divorce or separation, it's insane to attempt it. Boundaries must be obvious to all in order not to give the kids, your former partner, or extended family a false hope of reconciliation. It helps to keep alcohol to a minimum. My family has been celebrating the holidays together for years now. We include everyone, from Sharyl and her divorced parents to Larry, his father, and his father's new partner (Larry's mother has passed) to the combined yours-mine-and-ours kids.

But it hasn't always been that way. We have the typical stories of juggling Thanksgiving dinners. One year the kids had to leave our home right in the middle of dinner to get to Sharyl's home on time. It was very nerve-racking and made everyone edgy as we anticipated their departure. On the other hand, at Sharyl's house nothing could really start until the kids arrived, so they were frustrated, too. There were aspects to the two-home scenario that the kids *did* like. For one thing, they got double presents—some from Mom and some from Dad, some from new partners, and then the new partners' relatives heaped tons of presents on them, too. But for the adults the holidays were just one more reminder that they were divorced. Although we worked very hard to make the holidays happy for the kids, we dreaded them.

Finally, after years of two-home holidays, Melanie (Sharyl's daughter and my bonusdaughter) asked if we would consider having Thanksgiving dinner all together at her mom's house. Our first reaction was "Huh?" But when we thought about it we had to admit that we had grown to the point where we weren't uncomfortable being in one another's presence, so we decided to do it. Since we always try to put the kids first, and Melanie was asking, we took her request seriously. Sharyl, Larry, and I discussed it first and then asked the other kids how they would feel about it. Everyone voted yes, and so at about three o'clock Thanksgiving afternoon, we all congregated at Sharyl's home for the best Thanksgiving dinner in years. Sharyl made the turkey, and I made the mashed potatoes and gravy. To be honest, the first half hour was awkward, but the tension quickly melted away as we watched the kids chatting away at dinner. Melanie still says that our first time together was her favorite Thanksgiving, even though we've been celebrating together—trading houses each year—ever since.

I will always remember that when Larry and I were leaving Sharyl's home Melanie followed us out the door. She wrapped her arms around my neck and whispered in my ear, "Thank you. You've made me very happy." At that point there was no question we had done the right thing for our family.

Celebrating a Holiday Without the Kids

I certainly remember the first holiday I spent alone after my divorce. It was New Year's Eve, and my daughter was scheduled to spend the holiday with her dad, so I decided to celebrate with friends at a World Beat concert. The festival brought different countries together, comparing their foods, native dances, and the ways each celebrated the new year. It was held in an amphitheater, and there were so many things going on at once that I decided to stand at the top and look down so I could enjoy everything. As my eyes surveyed the chaos below, I saw my ex-husband, his girlfriend, and my little six-year-old daughter all dancing to the music. I'd had no idea they would be there, and I wanted to run down and scoop her up in my arms. But out of respect for my ex-husband's time with our daughter, I didn't budge. It was my first true realization that my daughter had a full and complete life with her dad. Our life together was not the only life she knew.

How do you celebrate holidays, which are so often centered on children, without children? Try to establish a new, alternative tradition for those times when the kids are not with you—something you can look forward to that will help alleviate any sadness you might feel. For example, the first holiday my husband and I spent together after we married was a very lonely time for us. The kids were scheduled to be with their other parents, and we were very bitter about the whole arrangement. On the spur of the moment, our best friends asked us to their home on Christmas Eve, along with other "displaced" people who were either single or divorced or a little bit crazy. We ate, drank some holiday cheer, and tried to forget that our children weren't coming home for a few days. The next year it was our turn to have the kids, and we had a conventional Christmas, but the following year, when the kids were with the other parents, we again spent Christmas Eve with our crazy friends. It became our "No Kids Holiday Tradition." It was fun and something we eventually looked forward to.

Of course, one alternative is for *no one* to be without the kids on the holiday. How? In our case, our kids soon started wondering just what was going on at our friends' home that was so much fun. So one Christmas when everyone was old enough, and it was our turn to have the kids, we decided to take them with us. We all assumed Sharyl would be alone for Christmas that year, but upon walking into our friends' home, there was Sharyl, standing in the kitchen. I was surprised, to say the least, but I joked with my friend, "OK, I can't believe you invited my husband's ex-wife to Christmas Eve." He ignored my joke and under his breath said, "We did that for you." You see, he knew firsthand of our growing pains in becoming a bonus-family and had looked for a way to help us give our kids the best holiday we could. After the initial shock wore off, I realized that we were—once again—in the midst of modifying a holiday tradition. Since that day, we all celebrate Christmas Eve together at our friends' house every year. It has become our new bonusfamily tradition.

The key to spending a holiday without the kids is to look for alternatives that make you happy—that don't remind you of what you can't do but reinforce what you can. And, as time goes on, don't be afraid of change. Be open to creating the holiday that works best for your family.

Gift Giving

When people divorce and remarry, gift giving at holidays gets really complex. Rather than decreasing, the number of presents you may be required to give can actually grow, and you may find yourself buying presents for people you never would have dreamed you'd be buying them for.

Gift Giving Between Exes

Whether or not you give your ex a gift at holiday time depends on the state of your relationship, of course, but also on whether either of you has remarried. It is unlikely that a new husband or wife would feel comfortable with a gift exchange between exes, so if one or both now has a new partner, then the answer would be no.

Offering a small present such as a candle or holiday candy *to the new couple*, however, is acceptable, as long as it is easily recognized as a gesture of goodwill. No presents that would remind the ex of your days together: no scrapbooks of the years gone by or videos showing your old photos with "your song" playing in the background. Those are completely inappropriate because they seem obvious ploys to reconcile with your ex or upset the new partner. Even from the start, which, quite frankly, surprised me, Sharyl bought my husband

EX-ETIQUETTE FOR HOLIDAYS

and me a little present for Christmas. It was usually something like dried fruit or a bottle of wine, but it was the thought and the gesture that helped pave the way to better communication all year round. Because she had set the example, we soon reciprocated. Each year I take some great pictures of her kids, put them in a frame that I know she would like, and present it to her from Larry and me. She has them all hanging in her home.

Buying Presents "From the Kids"

"My husband travels for business, and he won't be back until Christmas Eve. He has two older children from his previous marriage, and we have one together. His kids will spend Christmas this year with their mother. Yesterday my husband called and said he's too busy, could I please take his kids to buy their mother a gift? Is he kidding me? Because of their custody arrangement, I do talk to her, but it is strained at best. What would you suggest I do?"

I suggest you pack the kids up and head to the mall. It's not a new spouse's responsibility to buy presents for their spouse's ex, but there may be times when it is necessary. I don't offer this advice without knowing firsthand that it's not easy. There have been many times when Sharyl and I have bought each other presents "from the kids" and wondered what the heck we were doing. But, over the years, we have found that promoting a positive relationship with a child's parent or bonusparent only reinforces your relationship with that child.

Plus, if your relationship with the children's mother is strained, buying a present for her from the kids will do a lot to mend fences. With their dad gone, she'll know exactly who took her children out to buy her that present. Without your saying a word, she'll understand that it took you time and effort and that you had to say nice things about her in order to get the kids to start thinking about what kind of gift their mom might like. If there was ever a time to eat humble pie, it's when you realize that your spouse's ex or your ex's new partner took the kids out to buy you a present.

If, after all is said and done, you still can't bring yourself to take the kids to buy a Christmas present for their mother, then enlist help from another family member. Ask a grandparent, a sister-in-law, or a good friend to do it for you. But I have to say, if you don't do it yourself, I think you are missing an important opportunity to bond with your bonuskids and to make peace all around. Kids are not the only ones who learn by example. Welcome to the wonderful world of divorce and remarriage—bonus style.

> *"My fiancé's ex-wife has primary custody of their school-aged son, whom my fiancé sees every other weekend. His ex believes that she and my future husband should not purchase gifts for each other, which is understandable, but she extends this rule to gifts 'from' their son. This means that my fiancé has never received a gift from his son, who is too young to buy one himself. His ex has remarried, and I think her husband must be taking care of gifts 'from' her son at their house. I have never heard of this 'rule.' Is this common? If not, is there anything you advise that might change the situation?"*

There is no rule stating that you shouldn't buy a gift together with your child that is for your ex and "from" your child together. In fact, it's the sensitive thing to do, especially if your ex is still single. This mother is obviously coming from an old-school divorce state of mind in which people feel justified severing all ties once divorced.

Unfortunately, noncustodial parents may unknowingly contribute to this state of affairs. If your fiancé has never taken his child out to buy a present for his mom, then the mom may not recognize her responsibility either and may view her ex's lack of involvement as an indicator of what he expects from her. As much as your fiancé may hate the thought, it sounds like he might have to be the first one to reach across the line drawn in the sand to improve communication. Since the mother has primary custody and has remarried, without better communication between her and the father, it will be easy for him to end up as an afterthought—someone the child merely visits on the weekends—because his existence is not reinforced by the custodial parent. But if he initiates a cooperative attitude concerning gift giving during the holidays (e.g., "Let's coordinate our efforts for the holidays this year so Johnny gets exactly what he wants/needs for Christmas"), then when Christmas, birthdays, and Father's Day roll around, Mom may realize it's *her* obligation to go shopping with the child for a gift for Dad. If the father initiates some sort of gift-giving coordination, and the mother still refuses to buy presents for him from the child, you may have to step up to the plate. If you don't see that as your obligation, then perhaps another relative can fill in.

It is important to note that when a present is purchased by a parent for a parent, part of the ritual should be that the child accompanies the parent or bonusparent to buy the present. Many people faced with holiday stress or a desire to just get it over with simply buy a present and say, "I bought this for you to give your dad or mom." That really doesn't teach a child how to purchase a present for a loved one. A parent who takes a child out to buy a present for the other parent is teaching the child to be unselfish and consider others. It also affords the opportunity to discuss the other parent's likes and dislikes and to bond during conversation. Finally, it demonstrates firsthand that even though the child's parents are divorced, they both continue to love the child and respect each other. That is the best gift of all.

"Should I make the kids use their own money to buy presents for their father?"

If you have older children who receive an allowance, then having them use their own money to buy presents for others teaches them responsibility and reinforces that it is better to give than to receive. Make sure you have the correct motivation, though. Don't make the kids buy the gift just because you don't want to use any of *your own* money to buy your ex a present. Parents—biological and bonus—have to be bigger than that.

"When is it not appropriate to take the kids out to buy presents for their other parent?"

It may not be appropriate to support interaction between parent and child when the child is estranged from the parent for the following reasons:

- The parent's behavior is unpredictable because of addiction to drugs or alcohol, and the child's safety is at risk.
- The parent has exhibited past violent behavior toward the other parent or the child.
- The parent has committed a crime against the child.
- The parent is mentally ill and refuses treatment; seeing the parent in such a state would be upsetting to the child.

In other words, interaction should not be initiated with a parent whose behavior makes the child uncomfortable or has been determined to be detrimental to the child. When in doubt, you should always check with a professional who is familiar with the family's case.

Presents for Former Family

It's not uncommon for divorced people to expect their relatives to sever ties with their ex-spouse after the breakup. When a relative—

especially if it's a parent—wishes to continue the relationship, the divorced person feels betrayed. As a result, parents and extended family may resort to secretly maintaining a relationship with the ex, and when discovered, this can wreak havoc on family relations.

When considering such matters as whether to continue to buy presents for your ex's side of the family, try rephrasing the question to put the children first. Remove *yourself* from the scenario and use the children and their relationships with various "ex-relatives" as the criteria for your decisions. For example, the issue presented above could also be seen as whether it is proper to continue giving holiday gifts to your children's grandmother, uncles, aunts, and cousins after your divorce. Now, looking at it like that, what do you think your answer would be?

The relatives in question are only "ex" to you. Their relationship with your children remains the same even after the divorce. If, after the divorce, you choose to maintain a cordial relationship with former extended family, which, quite frankly, seems more appropriate than severing ties, then of course it is proper to give gifts to anyone you choose.

Many divorced people become upset when members of their immediate family secretly continue to meet with their ex. For example, perhaps a child, his father, and his grandfather on his mom's side go on a fishing outing every year. The divorced mother knows that her son is going away with his father, but she has no idea that her own father is joining them. When the child comes home one year with stories of the one that got away from Grandpa, his mom is shocked. Keeping the trip a secret was done in an effort to keep her discontent to a minimum, but what it actually did was make things even more complicated. That's when I hear, "I can't believe my own father chose him over me." But choosing one over the other wasn't the issue. The mother's ability to deal with the situation rests with her ability to allow the individual relationships to continue to exist separately and on their own merits—not necessarily in relation to her. With this in mind, you should feel free to offer gifts to former family if you or your child continues to interact with them in any capacity after the divorce.

Juggling Past and Present Partners

The Christmas holidays aren't the only times that divorced families face problems with holiday planning and celebrations. They *are* the holidays that carry the most anticipation, but other holidays, such as Easter or even Halloween, also have traditions associated with them that cause divorced families some concern. Any time you have to juggle past and present, there are logistical problems, as you will see from the following e-mail from a visitor to the Bonus Families Web site.

> *"My ex and I have been divorced for three years. We have always been cordial, but now I have someone new in my life, and it makes organizing any holiday difficult. The kids' father and I have continued to have Easter brunch together as a family, and then the kids look for Easter eggs out in the front yard. Now I would like to spend these special days with my new boyfriend and include his son, and I don't know how to handle it. I'm afraid my ex will get angry. I didn't give him much time to prepare for a change, and I know he's planning on showing up here for Easter brunch and our yearly egg hunt. What is proper ex-etiquette?"*

There are a few reasons why people choose not to tell someone something. First, out of fear—they may be afraid to make someone angry. Second, out of guilt—they may worry that they will hurt his or her feelings. Third, out of spite—they out and out know they are doing something wrong and they just want to do it anyway without considering or telling the other person. So, in response to any one of these reasons, you drag your feet, make excuses, and bring on far more problems for yourself than if you were just honest and straight-forward—ex-etiquette rule number eight. Following this rule almost always eliminates the difficulties of juggling past and present partners.

There is always a period of adjustment after a breakup as the couple transitions from the way they related in the past to how they will relate now and in the future. This transition time actually seems to be longer for those who have had an amicable divorce. Because there is minimal anger and resentment, there is no rush to sever emotional ties. Some unintentionally send mixed messages—such as that it may not *really* be over—because they are afraid of the ex's reaction, so they play down their dating. Then when someone new enters the picture, the ex feels blindsided and becomes angry.

If you haven't given your ex much time to make the emotional transition to your new relationship, then springing a change on him only days before the holiday is not good ex-etiquette. With this in mind, this year may not be the year to invite someone new. Start the transition from past to present now, and by next year, using the rules of good ex-etiquette as your guide, it will be easier to organize the holidays.

If you feel you *must* invite your new partner, keep in mind that holidays like Easter and Christmas usually offer multiple opportunities to get together. For example, keep your past family tradition going by having your ex and the kids to Easter brunch and the Easter egg hunt. Wind down the festivities in the early afternoon, and ask your new boyfriend and his son to join you for Easter dinner.

The Jewish Holidays

The Jewish New Year begins in mid- to late September. Most worship for two days in synagogue and share festive meals at home. Yom Kippur, or the Day of Atonement, follows a week later. It is observed with a day of fasting and worship. Hanukkah is the celebration of the triumph of the Maccabees (Jews) over Greek persecution and is celebrated for eight days. Passover is traditionally celebrated around the beginning of April. The celebration lasts for eight days, with the first two days and last two days celebrated as full festivals by Orthodox and Conservative Jews; Reform Jews observe Passover for only seven days. All Jews mark the first two days with seders, or formal dinners. The intervening days are known as "festival weekdays." Observant Jews usually go to synagogue to worship on the first two days and last two days of the holiday. Because several Jewish holidays are celebrated over more than one day, divorced parents may have some unique opportunities for compromise and flexibility when it comes to sorting through ex-etiquette issues.

Maintaining Jewish Holidays and Faith After Divorce

"When my ex and I were married we followed our Jewish faith, and so did our children. She has remarried someone of the Protestant faith and no longer observes the High Holidays—nor does she expect it of our two sons. I would like my boys to resume observing their faith and join my side of the family during Passover this year, but the holiday does not fall during my time with my children. I am afraid their religious heritage will be lost. How can I make sure my sons continue to observe their faith without undermining their mother's choices?"

Holiday celebrations can be even more problematic when a divorced parent remarries someone of a different faith, or when one person wishes to return to a previous faith after divorce. However, if you and your ex originally agreed to raise your children in a particular faith, then after divorce good ex-etiquette suggests that the children continue to be raised in that agreed-upon faith. Your ex has remarried someone of a different faith, but whether she converts or not, it is still her moral responsibility to uphold the original agreement. (If both of you had agreed to move away from the original religion, then the agreement could be changed.)

It is important to note that an abrupt change in a parent's religious practices can be very confusing to children already reeling from divorce. It helps, especially if the children are adolescents or teens, to formally explain to them why you have made the choice to worship differently from what you did when married to the child's mother or father. This should be preceded by a discussion with the other parent as to how the explanation should be handled. Then, using words like the following might be helpful: "I was raised (Christian, Jewish, Buddhist, etc.), and as things began to calm down after the divorce, following (Christianity, Judaism, Buddhism, etc.) seemed comfortable to me, and it is the choice I've made as an adult."

Parents should not attempt to change a child's religious identity after divorce, especially one they helped to create during the marriage. Mindful parents will demonstrate through words and deeds that they continue to respect the child's current religion, support the child's participation in religious celebrations, and attend the child's milestone events. This attitude will calm a confused child and appease the other parent's concern that the ex may attempt to undermine the faith in the eyes of the child. However, your ex's religion must be respected as well. A good alternative, enabling the children to experience both points of view, might be to separate the holidays along religious lines. Since the Jewish holidays of Passover and Hanukkah are celebrated around the same time as the Christian holidays of Easter and Christmas, but not on the same day, you and your ex could split up those days and each celebrate however you see fit. That way the kids will not lose their Jewish faith but will also learn about and respect their mother's new religion. You will have to look for compromises so that your children can continue to thrive in the religious lifestyle they knew before the divorce.

Passover Seders

Since Passover is celebrated over eight days with two formal seders, divorced Jewish parents may have an obvious compromise at hand: one parent hosts the seder on the first night, and the second hosts the seder on the second night. This way, children may celebrate the holiday with both of their parents but in their separate homes on different nights. However, it's not uncommon for Jewish families (especially those outside of the United States) to celebrate only one of the two seders during the holiday. In addition, because the Jewish tradition is to celebrate the holidays with several generations of family, divorced Jewish parents may occasionally find themselves hosting former in-laws or even a past partner if custody of the children is shared.

A friend of mine tells a story about the last time she attempted to invite all the "steps" to a Passover seder. The guest list included her children from a previous marriage, her mother and stepfather, her father and stepmother, her mother's parents, plus her husband's father and stepmother. It was, she reported, unbelievably stressful, particularly for the elderly grandparents, who were not used to combining past and present and had a difficult time being in the same room with her ex-husband. "My grandparents took sides after our divorce and never wanted to see him again, whereas I learned to move on for the sake of our children."

As in my friend's case, divorced parents are not always the ones responsible for the tension felt during the holidays. It's often relatives who feel they have a right to be part of the family's holiday decision-making process who create the additional tension. If extended family is to continue to participate in family holiday celebrations after a divorce, it's important to encourage them to demonstrate family unity through their words and actions, not to further sever family ties. Do not be afraid to put them on notice, reminding them that a child's parents are not the only ones that children look to as role models; a child's memories of the holidays are dependent on the feelings *all* family members create while celebrating. You can certainly set the example, however. The more you can cooperate with your child's other parent, the more you will reduce your stress and the stress experienced by your child.

Hanukkah

Hanukkah is the celebration of the triumph of the Maccabees (Jews) over Greek persecution in 165 B.C. Once victorious, the Jewish army rededicated the temple (the word *hanukkah* means "dedication"), but they were unable to find enough oil to light the menorah, or candleholder, to be used in the service. The Maccabees found only one bottle of oil, enough for a single night. But miraculously the oil lasted eight nights. That is why the holiday is celebrated over eight days. Each night a candle is lit and a prayer is said to commemorate the miracle. Small Hanukkah gifts may be offered to family and friends. Because the holiday spans eight days, divorced Jewish parents often split the days equally—four days with Mom, four days with Dad. Of course, like the other holidays mentioned, divorced families can also switch between Mom's house and Dad's house every year.

The thing that it is important to stress is not necessarily how easy it is to split the days of Hanukkah between divorced parents but that in the spirit of mutual love for your children, all parents attempting to co-parent after divorce must look for the compromise that will create the most loving holiday memories possible. How they do that will be different for each family, based on where they are in their own personal timeline after divorce. Some may be able to eventually celebrate together. Others may never be able to. The key to the right decision for your family is the same in all situations—the first rule of good ex-etiquette: Put the children first.

Holiday Photographs

More than simply a record of an event, family photos become some of our most cherished possessions. In years past, where to place family members in the photos was never really a problem. Stick Mom and Dad or Grandma and Grandpa in the middle and surround them with other family members. It made a great picture. Everyone was related, and everyone viewing the pictures knew who everyone was. Add divorce and remarriage, and suddenly new family members appear. Friends view your photos and you hear comments like, "Wait a minute, whose child is this?" or "That doesn't look like your sister."

The placement of family members in bonusfamily holiday photos, such as on Christmas cards, should easily communicate relationships. Place the children at the side of their biological parent, and place children shared by the parents between their parents. Obviously, lining everyone up in a straight line does not make for the best pictures. It's better to get creative, use different levels, perhaps have some people sitting and some standing.

Halloween

Halloween is a holiday that many divorced parents forget to list in their divorce decree when they're dividing up the kids' time. It just doesn't seem that important at the time. But Halloween is often children's favorite holiday, and it's not uncommon for moms and dads to dress up and go trick or treating right along with the kids. After divorce, you have to decide *who* goes with the kids, or if there's to be a neighborhood party, whose neighborhood?

Sharyl and her kids' Halloween ritual was always to congregate at the home of one of Sharyl's best friends for a pumpkin-carving party. After I came into the picture and my daughter was being raised as a sibling to Sharyl's children, she was invited to the party. I was nominated to take the kids to the party in their costumes (which I had sewn), and Sharyl would attend after work. All the moms stayed at the party with their children, and therefore I stayed with mine, but since the others were all Sharyl's friends, I was pretty uncomfortable. But I'm a great actress. Around 5:15, when Sharyl showed up, I was acting like I had no trouble with the whole thing: "And where's the next pumpkin you want me to carve?"

Sharyl walked in and was greeted by her buddies, only to see her daughter and my daughter dressed in darling little matching 1950s poodle skirts and little white shirts with pink puffballs hanging from their perfectly coiffed ponytails. Her daughter and my daughter began to spin excitedly, demonstrating the ease with which the little skirts spun around. Sharyl can't sew a stitch.

Needless to say, neither of us could wait to get out of there.

Did the kids know that we were squirming and shaking in our boots? I hope not, and they both kept those silly little skirts to play dress-up in for years. We pass on this story to anyone who questions whether we truly always got along. We didn't. It has been a slow process, but the true bridge to our friendship has been motherhood. When we left the labels of "first wife" and "second wife" behind and started relating to each other as mothers, that's when we realized the importance of getting along. Motherhood became the common ground on which our friendship has been built.

In order to help divorced parents get their perspective when sharing custody, I like to point out that it's not about "your time" or "their mother's time." All of it is your *child's* time, and that's what you have to consider. Where would the kids rather be? If most of their friends live in one parent's neighborhood, then making them trick-or-treat in the other parent's neighborhood, just because Mom and Dad can't get over themselves, seems selfish to say the least. If you all can't go out together, then pick the neighborhood you know the children would prefer, and let them have their good time with the parent who lives in that neighborhood. Your ex and his or her new partner might have a little more time with your child this particular week, but it will all come out in the wash.

We caution you against coming out and asking the kids where they would like to be. That forces kids to choose between their mom and dad, often right in front of them, and there will be no right answer they can give.

"My ex has a new girlfriend who has kids about the same age as ours. He thinks Halloween would be a great time to introduce her and get all the kids together and go trick or treating. What do you think?"

Holidays, especially holidays involving specific family traditions (such as trick or treating with the neighbors or stringing popcorn for the Christmas tree) are not good times to *introduce* new girlfriends or boyfriends for the first time. And if your prospective new partner has a child, that makes it twice as bad. You may think they'll get along just fine—and they may—but more often than not it registers with the kids that there's new competition encroaching on their family territory, threatening their family tradition. Better to set aside an afternoon for the first meeting, and keep it light—miniature golf, bowling, something to engage the kids so they remember having fun at their first meeting and look forward to a second one. Ease into it, for the kids' sake. Halloween can eventually be a great time to combine family fun; it's just not a good time to make the first introduction.

Mother's Day and Father's Day

Mother's Day and Father's Day may be two of the most challenging days on the calendar for divorced parents. Ironically, Mother's Day began as a day of peace in the United States. In 1870, overcome by the suffering experienced by both sides during the Civil War, social activist Julia Ward Howe wrote a proclamation suggesting that mothers come together to stop conflict. She couldn't have anticipated that her day of peace would someday actually initiate conflict for divorced parents. Sharyl and I have experienced it firsthand. Sharing the day does not come naturally. Fathers have reiterated the same message.

The problem arises when moms and bonusmoms or dads and bonusdads (counterpartners) both want to spend time with the kids on the same day. That's when sharing a day like Mother's Day or Father's Day becomes nearly impossible. All the insecurities associated with co-parenting rise to the surface. Mothers and fathers fear that their children might secretly prefer spending time with their bonusparent. Bonusparents must secretly acknowledge that they are not and never will be their bonuschild's biological parent. Things get even stickier in the case of children scheduled to be with their mother on Father's Day or their father on Mother's Day. Fear of "losing time" with the child provokes worried parents who feel a little insecure about their position to not want to cooperate. It is important for each parent to strive to support the other parent's attempt to parent their child appropriately. I specifically call this to the attention of parents who demand strict adherence to visitation schedules without weighing the true impact of what they are asking.

The rules of good ex-etiquette suggest that all parent figures look for ways to help the children in their care spend the day with the appropriate parent. If this is impossible because the child's dad or mom lives a great distance away, the custodial parent should make an effort to support the child in buying a card, sending a present, or making a phone call to wish the other biological parent a happy Father's Day or Mother's Day. Of course, if you're dealing with a flaky ex who rarely shows up for visitation days or is not in the child's life, suggesting that the child send a card or present may actually be detrimental to his or her self-esteem. Hinting to a child that Dad or

Mom doesn't really care certainly won't help the child feel more secure. That's when the attention of a doting bonusparent is particularly important.

> *"My two young sons live with me most of the time and have become close to their stepfather. Father's Day is coming up, and my ex wants to see his sons that day. But it falls on my weekend, and I would like the boys to spend time with my husband celebrating the day as a family."*

Society tells us that the best possible family scenario is the nuclear family—Mom, Dad, and kids all together, and many of us strive for that even though our previous choices (divorce or separation) actually prevent it from ever being true. In response to the guilt they feel about getting divorced, some parents, when they remarry, attempt to re-create the nuclear family. But it's not a nuclear family, it's a bonus-family, and all the parental figures must put their guilt aside and work together in the best interests of all the children in their care.

Ex-etiquette rule number ten is "Compromise whenever possible." And there is a compromise here if you and your ex look for it. For example, if your ex lives nearby, perhaps the boys could spend the morning and afternoon with their dad and then return to your house for a bonusfamily Father's Day dinner. Or, even though it's your weekend, you may want to consider letting the boys spend the weekend with their dad but ask him to return by noon on Sunday so the bonusfamily can observe the day together. Or they can spend Father's Day with their biological dad and make the next Sunday "Bonusdad's Day." Start a new bonusfamily tradition. There *is* a compromise. There is always a compromise. You, your husband, and your ex just have to remove your own interests from the decision-making process, then you will find it.

"My son likes to give two Mother's Day gifts—one for his mom and one for his bonusmom. Last year his mom found out and was really upset. This year his class is making baskets for Mother's Day, and my son wants to make two. Should I discourage him from making one for my wife? She loves him very much."

When children like their bonusparents, it's because all of the adults in the picture have done something right. Giving them permission to form a loving bond with their bonusparent or to openly discuss their love for their mom or dad makes for happy, secure children and eliminates those gut-wrenching allegiance issues that make kids feel that caring for one betrays the other.

With any luck, your ex is doing whatever she can not to act hurt in front of her son. If she does show her wounded feelings, she'll make him feel as if he is doing something wrong, when he's just doing what he was taught to do—to care for someone who treats him with love and respect. With that in mind, I don't think you should discourage your son from making two baskets. You should take note, however. If your ex is reacting this strongly, it may be a sign that you have downplayed her importance. This often happens when parents remarry and are trying to establish their new family. If that's what has happened at your house, fix it. Fast. You'll be surprised how quickly his mom's attitude changes.

Valentine's Day

In the past Valentine's Day was a day to profess your love in a romantic way. Over the years the tradition has changed somewhat in that parents and children may also exchange cards or trinkets that offer a sentimental "I love you."

"My ex and I are quite friendly. Even though he has remarried, people are often amazed that we are divorced. We have a lot of history—some bad, but some very good, and this time of year, when I'm handing out Valentine's cards to our adult kids, I wonder if I should include a card or a little present for him, for old times' sake?"

First, it's important to congratulate you on your ability to stay cordial for the kids' sake. Now that they are adults, the fact that their parents can comfortably interact will make it much easier on them when they marry and have children. Because you two can interact easily, there will be no need for separate birthday parties or holiday celebrations for the grandkids.

That said, your ex has remarried, and his wife is his valentine. Giving him a Valentine's Day card is inappropriate. I understand that you may both have bittersweet memories of your times together, but that doesn't give you the right to disrespect your ex's new marital union. Ask yourself this question: would you give him this card or gift in secret, or while he was standing next to his wife? Most likely, it would be one of those secret little things you might do with a wink. If a gesture is not something you would do right in front of his wife, then that's a sign that it is inappropriate. Now that you are divorced, your responsibility to each other is as parents—not former lovers. Not unless you plan on picking up the pieces when he gets his next divorce—which is just plain tacky. So keep those sentimental cards to yourself. That's good ex-etiquette.

However, here's a note for those who are divorced and neither person has remarried. If you would like to give your ex a card or present on Valentine's Day, you should think about the potential consequences—not just between you and your ex but how knowledge of your gesture might affect your children.

3

Ex-Etiquette for New Arrivals, Birthdays, and Other Milestone Events

"Your children need your presence more than your presents."
—Jesse Jackson

Milestone events such as the birth of a new baby, birthdays, and graduations take on new meaning for bonusfamilies. A new baby affects many more people than just the nuclear family of times past. Divorced parents, kids, former family, and bonusparents all have a role to play and may wonder what that role should be. Children's birthday parties can become logistical nightmares. Confirmations and graduations can become times of stress and avoidance rather than celebration.

This chapter looks for alternatives to what was once regarded as the norm and discusses new attitudes and new rules of behavior for integrating past and present when facing these and other milestone events.

New Arrivals

Having a new baby after divorce raises so many issues. What's the best way to tell your children about the new baby? What is their relationship to the baby? How will your ex handle the news? Who comes to the baby shower? Keeping the rules of good ex-etiquette in mind will ensure that this is a time of joy and growth for your family.

Preparing Your Children for Their New Sibling

Remarried parents often ask me how to help their children accept the arrival of a new baby. This takes some careful planning, and even though you may think you are doing everything right, it's easy to overlook the obvious. I found this to be true in my own home. My husband and I did everything the "experts" suggest. We talked about the baby before it was born. We encouraged the children to express their feelings about the baby. My best friend let the kids help plan the baby shower, which they attended. We bought books that had beautiful pictures of how the baby was developing.

That's when my daughter Anee dropped the bomb. Soon after the baby was born, I was sad to learn that after all that preparation she still feared that I would love the new baby more. Her reasoning, at nine, was that since I was married to the baby's daddy and not her daddy, I would love the new baby more. As I thought about it, I could see how those feelings could foster resentment of the new baby, me, even her bonusdad. I had tried so hard to help this family gel, but there always seemed to be something I overlooked.

My bonuskids had similar feelings. Although we had a great relationship, other relatives with misguided intentions had warned them that I would have little time for them after the baby was born. They were told that everything would change. Although outwardly they were excited, inside they were frightened that this new life they had finally grown used to was going to change yet again.

Here are some ways to help your bonusfamily adjust to the addition of a new baby:

- **Encourage your children to talk about their feelings regarding the new arrival as much as possible.** Don't become impatient with a child who admits to being angry or sad or jealous for these feelings (e.g., "How can you say that about your baby sister?!"). You'll only make the child feel guilt on top of anger and jealousy. Do your best to redirect those negative feelings into positive ones. For example, if the child says, "You love the new baby more than me," your response could be, "Honey, you are both so different." Then pick out something at which the existing child excels. In my case, my daughter was a great little artist. So I could say, "How many people do you think can draw as well as you can? Here are some pens and paper. Please draw me a picture to hang in my office. Every time I look at the picture I will think of your smiling face. And I just love you to pieces."

- **Try not to make changes that the older child will equate with the new baby's arrival.** In other words, don't preface a big change with "Now that the baby's here, you get the big-girl bed." A child may be inclined to think the reason for the change is that the new baby has come to live at her house; this might make her resent the baby. Most changes, such as going to preschool or moving from a crib to a bed, are age related and should be presented as such—not in relation to the baby's arrival.

- **Be careful that the new baby does not dominate the lives of the older children.** Many parents, especially those who have a large combined family, expect the older children to help rear their child. That's the quickest way to breed resentment in siblings—especially teenaged siblings. A new baby is the parents' responsibility, not that of the children. Don't expect older children to clean up after the baby. Don't immediately dump babysitting responsibilities on an adolescent. Until your children have accepted the new child as a member of the family, try to maintain a babysitting swap with other parents. Watch how much you ask grandparents to watch the baby, too; older children might start wondering why their grandparents prefer the new baby to them.

- **Look for ways to spend one-on-one time with your children.** Even though a new baby will take up most of your time, your biological kids and bonuskids still need private time with their parents and bonusparents. A great way to find "extra time" is to integrate the children into your everyday routine. Let Dad watch the baby while Mom takes the older child to the grocery store, or vice versa. When it's time to have the oil changed in the car, ask one of the kids to come along for company. Grab a quick bite together while you are waiting. Use the time to talk, hang out, and renew your bond. Talk about the things you like to do together.

- **Do what you can to enlist support from the older children's other parent.** Even if there is anger or possibly jealousy on the part of your ex or your spouse's ex, remind them that a positive word from them will go a long way to help make their child feel safe and secure.

Avoid the "Real Family Syndrome"

There's a trap that some divorced parents fall into—the "Real Family Syndrome." It starts with the concept of "I'm your *real* mother" or "I'm your *real* (biological) father, and anything over at that other house isn't quite as good. We're the authentic family—your *real* family." The parent implies that *this* house is real and everything at *that* house is not—and that includes new little half siblings or bonussiblings that the child may love. This type of parent is feeling insecure and wants the child to prefer being with him or her, without taking into account what this attitude actually does to the child. Convincing a child that he has no "real" connection with a half sibling or stepsibling does not help her sleep at night or ease her transition from one family to another. Telling a child that one household is the real family and the other is not might be compensation of some sort for a hurting, divorced parent who feels unloved or overlooked, but it only confuses the child. Sometimes siblings—be they bonus- or half siblings—have no real emotional connection to each other. They grow up in the same home merely tolerating each other. However, if there is a connection, and the bonus- or half sibling is a good influence on your child, then undermining that connection will not benefit either child.

The New Arrival and Your Ex

"Should I tell my ex that I'm having a baby?"

That depends on the state of your relationship. If you do not speak and have moved on, then the answer is no. Informing an ex that you are expecting when you have no current relationship could be misunderstood on many levels. You could be seen as bragging or complaining or even wanting him or her back. Taking that into consideration, say nothing to your ex and have a nice life.

If you have a relationship with an ex because you share children or perhaps a business after the breakup, then good ex-etiquette suggests that you should notify him or her well in advance of the birth of your child. Some people may find this to be a strange suggestion, but it is rooted in sound logic. If you share custody of the children, then your children are active members of two families—Mom's family and Dad's family. To successfully co-parent, both parents must be notified when an important event happens in either family so that the other parent can be supportive of the children during the change.

If you share a business, even if you don't see each other every day, even if you're just a silent partner, your presence (or lack thereof) still has an impact on the business. Exes should be treated the same as any other employee or employer, meaning that they should be notified of maternity or paternity leave as soon as possible so they can calculate how a leave of absence will affect the business.

"What is my role now that my ex, who is the father of my child, is having a new child?"

Your role is that of the mother or father of the existing child, and as a parent your job is to do what you can to make sure that your child does not fear being overlooked by the introduction of a new child. This is a huge responsibility. Many parents feel no obligation to prepare their child for the introduction of their ex's new child. They figure that this is the ex's responsibility. But this new child is going to be a half sister or half brother to your child. The children will interact with each other, and their relationship will be a link between homes.

If you see that your child is worried about the new arrival, saying things like "Don't worry Sweetie, you still have me" will probably not be much comfort. Of course, reassuring your child of your abiding love is always a good thing to do; however, you can really help your child with reassurances that the *other* parent's love will not diminish. *That's* good ex-etiquette—not giving in to typically vengeful behavior and instead doing what is right for the sake of your child. Do not use this time, even subtly, to reinforce the child's anxiety, believing that it will bring him or her closer to you. It may for the time being, but you are only achieving this goal at your child's expense, by reinforcing insecurity.

To ward off sibling rivalry, you and your ex may both want to offer your child a present when the new baby is born. Include a note stating how much you both love the child and expressing confidence that the child will be a terrific big brother or big sister.

New Arrivals and Former Family

New babies are certainly a blessing, but their arrival can raise difficult questions not only for the bonusfamily expecting the addition but also for the former family of one or both of the parents. Grandparents to one batch of children wonder if they should play the same role to their grandchildren's new half sibling. For example, say a woman has two children from her first marriage and is now expecting a baby with her new spouse. The parents of her ex-husband are her kids' grandparents, but what is their role vis-à-vis the new baby, who will be the half sibling of their biological grandchild but is no biological relation to them? When their grandkids come to visit them, do they exclude the kids' half sibling or treat him or her differently? Of course not. Good ex-etiquette suggests they welcome the new arrival with open and loving arms, doing whatever they can to support the new family and to make sure that the grandkids, biological or otherwise, don't feel awkward or tense about the situation.

This may not be easy for all former in-laws, especially if their son or daughter has died or if there was a particularly messy divorce. They may subconsciously feel some resentment toward their former daughter- or son-in-law either for moving on with life or for hurting their child in some way during the marriage or divorce, and that bitterness may even extend to a new child who is not *their* son or daughter's child. You would hope that those harboring these feelings will quickly realize that they can best honor their son or daughter by being loving grandparents to their son or daughter's kids, and that means accepting their grandkids' new siblings, being a positive role model, and making no differentiation between them at holidays—or any other time.

> *"I just received a birth announcement from my former son-in-law, to whom I have remained close after my daughter's passing. He has remarried and recently had a child. Should I send a present?"*

Many feel that when they receive a birth announcement a gift is expected in return. This is not true. Receiving an announcement does not obligate you to send a present. It is understandable that you have stayed close. Your past history as his mother-in-law does not dampen your desire for his now having a loving and happy life. So send a gift if you like, and add, "With sincere best wishes for the future." Make sure the card accompanying the gift is addressed to both your former son-in-law *and* his new wife and is meant "for the baby," not just for your former relation.

Announcing the New Arrival

Divorced people should feel free to send birth announcements, make phone calls, or tell in person anyone they would like to notify about the birth of a child. Announcements usually begin with an excited phone call to close family, starting with the family of the mother and then progressing to the family of the father.

Announcing to Divorced Parents

If the new mother's parents are divorced, the announcement call goes first to the parent who raised her. This means that if the mother was raised primarily by her mother, then her mother would receive the first phone call. If the child was raised primarily by her father, then he would receive the first phone call. If the child was raised equally by Mom and Dad, standard etiquette suggests that Mom is notified first. The same protocol is followed on the father's side of the family if the new father's parents are divorced. A more formal card sent through the mail—and now sometimes by e-mail—is often done as a follow-up.

Single-Mother Birth Announcements

If a mother has never married and is composing a formal birth announcement, she should include her first and last names. If the mother is recently divorced from the father of the child, the birth of the child is still a happy event, and it is still good ex-etiquette to send an announcement of birth. The announcements should not be signed "Mr. and Mrs." They should be signed using only the name the mother will use after the breakup. For example, when married the couple was known as Dave and Samantha Jones. The mother would now sign the announcement simply Samantha Jones, or using her maiden name if she has returned to that. If the father of the child passed away before the birth, the mother would sign the announcement Mrs. David Jones or possibly Samantha Jones but not Mr. and Mrs. David Jones.

Bonusfamily Birth Announcements

Bonusfamily birth announcements are a great way to promote family unity and reinforce a child's excitement about having a new half brother or half sister. Let the older child or children assist in picking out the announcements and addressing the envelopes. If they're too young to do that, perhaps have them stick the stamps on. Look for ways to get them involved.

The wording of a bonusfamily birth announcement would be something like:

> [half siblings' names] proudly introduce their new little brother/sister.

or

> [half siblings' names] would like you to meet their new baby brother/sister.

A bonusfamily birth announcement might say:

> **Bill and Michelle Callen and their combined children, Mica, Sue, and Robbie, announce with great joy the birth of Madeline Louise.**

Baby Showers

Bridal and baby showers originated years ago when people tended to marry and have children at a younger age and needed more help from their parents, extended family, or the community to get started in their life together. Many people marry and have children later in life now, but showers are still very much the tradition. Although they have changed somewhat along with the times, when someone is expecting, friends and extended family still gather together to offer the parents-to-be the necessary things for the baby.

Baby showers are most often given before the baby is born so that the parents-to-be can enjoy the gifts right away and will know what they still need once the baby arrives. Usual presents are baby clothes, diapers, toys—anything parents can use to help them get ready for baby. A mother adding a child to a bonusfamily may especially welcome these gifts. Although she may already have children from her previous marriage, it is likely that a few years have passed and she now needs things for the new baby.

"Who gives the baby shower?"

Traditional etiquette suggests that immediate family should not host a baby shower. The reason is that showers are parties at which people offer gifts, and it would appear self-serving if the expectant mother's mother threw a shower for her daughter. This is also true for the sister of the mother-to-be. A more appropriate choice would be close friends, sisters-in-law, or other extended-family members. Truthfully, immediate-family members often help behind the scenes and even offer their homes as the place the shower is to be held, but someone other than an immediate-family member should do the formal hosting and send invitations.

> "Over the years my former sister-in-law has become my best friend. She and my brother have two kids together, but they've been divorced for years, and now his new wife, with whom I am also friendly, is having a child. I would like to throw her a baby shower, but my former sister-in-law is having a fit. I just don't know what to do."

When a couple breaks up, it can be difficult to know how to divide the relatives and ex-relatives. Years ago things were more clear-cut: I get my side of the family; you get yours. But now that so many share custody of their children after divorce or separation, it's just not that easy. The kids go back and forth between the homes of their mom and dad, stay in contact with the other side of the family, and relationships continue that years ago might have been severed. That's when we face problems like the one described. Where should one's allegiance lie when a relative divorces?

Divorce cuts the ties between husband and wife but not the ties with extended family when the divorced couple has had children. Grandma is Grandma whether Mommy is married to Daddy or not. You are an aunt to all of your brother's children regardless of whom he is married to.

It is commendable not to have taken sides and to have continued to be friends with both women. If your brother's former wife was really a good friend, she would never have "had a fit," which in essence is asking you to choose between past and present family—an impossible choice that few would be able to do gracefully. It is simply unfair for a first spouse to expect her former in-laws' allegiance to the exclusion of their new relative. Your brother's new wife is the mate with whom you and other family members *must* interact now.

Under the circumstances, if you want to maintain friendships with your brother's first wife and also with his second wife, you may not want to host the shower all by yourself. You may want to enlist someone else to formally host the baby shower—perhaps another good friend, an aunt, or a cousin—and help with the festivities behind the scenes.

"Should I buy a gift for my ex's new baby?"

Presents for a new baby are always welcome; however, presents from an ex should be somewhat restrained in nature, and special attention should be given to offer the gift as a sincere gesture of your best wishes, never as a dig or to communicate "I told you so." There's a new child coming into this world, and with that you have the ability to wipe the slate clean and set a good example.

Appropriate presents would be baby blankets, rattles, or toys. It is not good ex-etiquette to offer a present that reminds the ex of your time together. It is appropriate, however, to return any of your ex's family heirlooms that you may still have, such as antique baby blankets or keepsakes that can be passed on to the new baby. If you and your ex have had children together, another nice way to welcome the ex's new baby is to offer the present from the new baby's big brother or sister.

"Should ex-wives be invited to baby showers?"

That depends on whose shower and whose ex-wife it is. If the first wife and second wife of the same man happen to travel in the same social circles and a shower is being held for a mutual friend, then they should both be invited. It is their choice whether to both attend. If the ex-wife in question is the first wife of the husband of the mother-to-be, however, it is likely that the mother-to-be will not feel comfortable with the first wife's attending, no matter how close they have become. Mothers discuss birth stories at baby showers, and this opens the conversation up to a discussion of the first wife's labor and delivery—not something the second wife may want to hear about, especially if her husband was in attendance.

The case is a little different if it is the first wife who has remarried and is now having another child. If the first and second wives get along and are successfully co-parenting any existing children, it is not inappropriate to invite the second wife, especially if the children will be in attendance. If the women have a positive relationship, the children may even ask why the bonusmom is not in attendance. Any invitation of this sort should, of course, be discussed with the first wife before the host issues the invitation.

Another time the first wife and the second wife may feel comfortable attending the same baby shower is when the shower is for their daughter or bonusdaughter. If both women have worked through any problems and can be in the same room comfortably, then it is appropriate that both attend. When my own daughter, Anee, has children, although Sharyl is technically no relation to her (Sharyl is Anee's bonussiblings' mother), I know Anee would be very disappointed if Sharyl did not attend.

To those who hold grudges: it is selfish to tell an expectant mother that you will not attend her shower if someone of whom you don't approve will attend. Giving ultimatums like "If she's going to be there, I'm not going!" when expectant mothers have enough stress to deal with is very bad ex-etiquette.

"Should baby showers be held for single mothers?"

Baby showers are celebrations designed to help new parents— whether never married, divorced, or widowed—prepare for the arrival of their child. So, using this as the criterion, of course baby showers should be held for single mothers. I believe this question is a holdover from an earlier era, when having a child outside of marriage was frowned upon. Today, over one-third of all babies born in the United States are born to single parents, so those old-school rules just don't apply. Look to a baby shower as an opportunity to celebrate a new arrival with friends and family and to offer your support for a happy life to the mother and child.

Baptisms and Christenings

A child is a symbol of a couple's bond, and most people would find it inappropriate for an ex of one of the new parents to attend the new baby's christening. However, in my work with Bonus Families I have actually met many families who would find it out of place *not* to invite the ex (and even include the ex in the ceremony as the godparent). That's because the ex is no longer regarded as an ex-spouse but as the respected mother or father of the co-parented children. I remember one time when my husband, our combined children, and I were planning a vacation. We had finally agreed on a date when my youngest daughter, Harleigh, who was seven or eight at the time, asked, "Can Sharyl get off work that week?" Everyone laughed, and she immediately understood why. Sharyl would not be going on a family vacation with us, but Harleigh's first inclination was to include her sister and brother's mother in the planning because that was all she had ever known.

Some families face a situation in which the older children from the first marriage were not baptized, but the couple has now decided—perhaps because it is more important to the second spouse—to baptize their new child. If the older kids are asking questions about this, then ex-etiquette rule number eight applies: "Be honest and straightforward." Using age-appropriate language, discuss different faiths and beliefs with your children and explain that your new wife or husband practices this particular faith and wants his or her child to participate in the rituals associated with the faith and to follow the faith as well.

I worked with one family who baptized all the kids—new baby and older half siblings—at the same time, a sort of "bonusfamily baptism." The ex-spouse did not oppose this decision and felt that it actually offered the children a way to bond with the new child. Work with your pastor, if he or she is willing, to make up your own bonusfamily baptism or christening ritual. Get creative. Special family rituals of this sort can unite the family.

Choosing Your Ex as Your Child's Godparent

A godparent in some denominations of Christianity is someone who sponsors a child's baptism and is responsible for the child's religious education and for caring for the child should he or she be orphaned. (It is important to remember, however, that godparent is not a legal status, and if the parents seriously intend the godparents to act as caregivers in case of their death, it should be specified in their will.) Some denominations of Christianity require prospective godparents to have been christened before they can take on this responsibility. The Roman Catholic Church also requires that the godparents have undergone confirmation. Today, appointing a godparent may not carry religious overtones as much as it is an opportunity for the parents to choose an individual to take a vested interest in raising a more complete human being.

Deciding who will raise your child if you cannot requires some serious soul-searching. It is rare that you co-parent as closely with a friend or relative as you would with an ex. We all have an idea of how our friends and relatives parent their kids, but we are usually not privy to the way they make decisions on a day-to-day basis. You do get that sort of insight when you co-parent with an ex-spouse, especially if you share custody equally and must interact on an almost daily basis. This is why I am no longer surprised when people tell me they have asked their ex or their ex's new partner to be a godparent to their newborn. Who better than someone you know loves your children as much as you do?

In our case, my husband's ex-wife, Sharyl, has been designated to watch over my minor daughter should something happen to my husband and me—much to my sister's dismay. There were many things to take into consideration when making this decision. My daughter has half siblings with whom she is very close, and my sister lives five hundred miles away. If something happened to my husband and me, our daughter would not only have lost her parents but she would have to move away from the only immediate family she has ever known. When you look at it this way, from the perspective of your kids' best interests, it begins to make sense how someone might choose their spouse's ex even over blood relatives to serve as godparent.

Ex-Etiquette for Grandparents and Bonusgrandparents

Grandparents and bonusgrandparents face some unique issues when there is a new arrival. What should a bonusgrandparent be called? What visitation rights do they have should their son or daughter pass away? How can divorced grandparents work together to support their child through the birth of their grandchild? Grandparents, too, can use the rules of ex-etiquette as a guide.

What to Call Various Grandparents

"Is there any etiquette rule regarding who gets the first choice in names for a grandparent? In our case, a stepgrandmother has chosen to be called the more familiar Nana before either biological grandmother had a chance to claim it!"

The problem described can truly set bonusfamilies on edge. Biological grandparents think, "Who does she think she is? She's not even the 'real' grandma, and she's already claiming the 'Nana' name!" The truth is that stepparents who have been around a long time may not even realize they're creating a problem. They may already have grandchildren who call them nana and just expect that's what the new grandchild will call them, too. But some people just plain don't want to share the grandparent distinction and resent having to do so. The problem is, in this day of divorce and remarriage, that there may be more than two people in the grandmother role and more than two in the grandfather role and not enough distinctive names to go around.

If a rule must be established for this problem, it would be that family names follow bloodlines, but I hope that no one would pull rank in this case and that the grandparents in question would look for other solutions that will set the stage for family problem solving in the future. Names for grandparents are usually chosen in one of two ways: they're either handed down from generation to generation or the family adopts the sound the little ones make when attempting to say "grandma" or "grandpa." At my house Grandma became "Me-Ma" when the oldest grandchild started calling her that as a baby. The grandmothers are either Me-Ma Helen or Me-Ma Donna. At Sharyl's house there are an abundance of grandmas—or people respected as grandmas—and their distinction is simply made by adding their first name after the word grandma: Grandma Grace, Grandma Donna, Grandma Betty. (Note that there is a Me-Ma Donna and a Grandma Donna—same Donna, it's just that the two different families use two different nicknames for her.)

Many people feel that the name the child uses for the grandparents will be what sets the grandparents apart from each other. That means there can be only one Nana or one Grandma. No one else can share the name. What will set grandparents apart from each other is how fun, kind, or loving they are, not their name. It may be time to release ownership of any particular title and look for other ways to make a difference. Grandparents can find their own niche and allow that to distinguish them from each other. They should decide what they are good at and offer that to the kids; that way the children will get the best of each grandparent, and names won't make a difference.

Grandparent and Extended-Family Visitation Rights

The question of family visitation rights usually comes into play when there has been a nasty divorce and custody battle, a parent dies, and the remaining parent wants to prevent the family of the deceased from seeing the child. Preventing visitation based on anger toward the deceased is certainly not in the child's best interests. Children are reeling after the death of a parent and need the comfort of everyone who cares about them. A good reason to prevent visitation, on the other hand, might be if the relatives are violent, mentally ill, or have troubles with drugs or alcohol.

Every state has a grandparent visitation statute that allows grandparents and other relations to ask for visitation rights in order to maintain their relationships with loved ones. Since divorce laws are different from state to state, it is always advisable to check with an attorney or family court services to verify the law. Grandparents who wish to file for visitation must do so in the area where their grandchild lives. For example, a grandparent who lives in Colorado but whose grandchild lives in California must file for visitation in the superior court in the county in California in which the grandchild lives.

There are some important stipulations to visitation rights. First, a relationship between the grandparent or relative and the child must already exist before the relative may petition for visitation. Second, any visits must be deemed in the child's best interests. Third, any visitation scheduled for relatives cannot interfere with the living birth parent's visitation rights.

When You and Your Ex Become Grandparents

"My adult daughter is pregnant. Her father and I barely talk, but we both want to be at the baby's birth. I don't think he and his wife should go. It will upset my daughter if there is arguing."

It is not uncommon for children of divorce to cultivate two strong but very separate relationships with their battling parents, playing down the importance of one when spending time with the other. Under such circumstances, it would not be surprising if a child also kept secret the bond developed with the stepparent. It only becomes evident to the parent when there is a milestone event in the child's life—a wedding, for example, when a father and stepfather are both asked to walk a daughter down the aisle or, in this case, the birth of a baby.

At first it sounds like your child's concerns are being put first. The logic seems to be, "If my ex goes, there will be arguing. Therefore, my ex should not be there for my child's sake." However, a parent should never be so presumptuous as to assume that he or she is the parent of choice. If your daughter truly feels that she can invite only one of her parents to her milestone event, then you and your ex have failed as parents. It is never a parent's place to suggest or imply that a child should take sides, even under the guise of looking out for the child's best interests. Your daughter might want both her mom's and dad's sides of the family present at the birth of her child. If you want to be a role model for your child and your child's children, you should strive to pass on a legacy of cooperation and compromise.

Children's Birthday Parties

It's difficult for some adults to recall how important birthday parties were to them as children. Kids anticipate their special day for weeks if not months. They want everything to be perfect, and they certainly do not want feuding parents embarrassing them in front of their friends. With a little thoughtfulness, planning, and cooperation, parents in just about any situation can ensure that their kids or bonuskids have a fun, memorable, and joyful birthday party.

One Party or Two?

When divorced parents plan a child's birthday party, the first question is typically whether there should be one party or two. If parents are estranged, it's usually best to opt for the two-party solution. Two separate parties ensure that there will not be a scene in front of the kids.

There are downsides to the two-party solution, however. It complicates the guest list and makes it difficult for the child to celebrate with everyone he or she loves at once. Which party will his friends attend? Will all of her cousins from both sides of the family be able to share her day? What about both grandmas and both grandpas? What typically happens is that one parent, say Mom, ends up giving the "friends' party" and possibly includes the relatives from her side of the family. Then Dad has another party and invites the relatives from his side of the family. If Mom's relatives cannot attend the friends' party, it's not uncommon to end up giving a child *three* parties—an additional party for the family members who could not attend the friends' party.

With all this juggling of family and friends, divorced parents have to do some soul-searching to determine whether they're really serving their child's best interests by insisting that they can't be in the same room and must throw separate parties.

Party Planning Guidelines

When planning a child's birthday party, divorced parents and bonusparents should ask themselves the following questions:

- Whose party is it?
- Will not inviting a certain person—specifically the child's other parent or bonusparent, grandparent, uncle, or other relative—make the child sad or appear to be an obvious snub?
- Where will the party be held?

Remember that it's your child's party, not yours. Therefore, you should invite the guests you think your child would like to invite. A child's birthday party is not the place to make a statement about whom you like and dislike. It's your job as a parent to provide a secure environment for your children and to teach them how to get along with someone in the face of conflict. For children's parties where exes are invited, it is best to choose neutral territory or a public place like a skating rink or pizza parlor—not the home of the parent hosting the party. Home is private territory, and having your child's party at your home may set an already uncomfortable ex-spouse and his or her new partner even more on edge. If this is obvious to the child, you have defeated the purpose of attempting to celebrate together.

Birthday Party Ex-Etiquette for Extended Family

"Each year we have birthday parties for my husband's grand-children and invite our side of the family. My stepson and his wife will also throw a party and invite both sides of the family. Is it wrong to not attend that party when we have already had one for our side? Neither my husband nor I feel comfortable being around his ex's family."

In a word, yes, it is wrong not to attend such a party. But more than that, other rules of good ex-etiquette were broken and need to be discussed. It's the mother and father's responsibility to throw their children's birthday parties, not the grandparents'. Of course there may be exceptions—perhaps the parents are strapped for cash and ask the grandparents for help. However, in most cases a grandparent, especially a bonusgrandparent, as in this case, should never throw a party for their grandchild *before* the child's parents without checking dates, confirming guest lists, and getting the parents' authorization.

Once invited, extended family, especially grandparents and their new partners (bonusgrandparents), should always attend parties for their grandchildren. Here's why. If you, as an adult child of divorce, host a party for your own child and invite your divorced parents and their new partners, plus other extended family, you are making a statement to everyone—especially to your children—that people who have disagreed in the past can put their issues aside for the sake of family. The parents of the child, in this case, are obviously looking for a way to set the example or perhaps remain neutral so that the entire extended family can unite for the sake of the child.

It is understandable that some relatives may feel uncomfortable in situations like this; nevertheless, it is important to be gracious and set an example for the children. A family member who is too uncomfortable to attend can decline the invitation with an honest explanation. But a better solution would be to plan a special birthday outing with the child on a day other than the child's birthday—and do your best not to discuss your discomfort with the child. But relatives, bonus or biological, should not hold another party. That usurps parental privilege and will only breed contempt and gossip among family members.

Coordinating Your Child's Birthday Gifts

"My ex and I both want to get our son the skateboard he wants for his birthday. How do we decide who gets to give it to him?"

Questions like this are typically asked when the divorced couple sees themselves as divorced individuals, not as co-parents to the same child. They are involved in a power struggle in which both parents want their child to like them better. Divorced parents of this kind will attempt to one-up each other by buying the children "better" presents or trying to entice the child to their home by getting puppies or the newest video games—they secretly gloat in their success when the child does not want to return to the other parent's home.

Divorced parents who put their children first approach gift giving from a united point of view. This means they either offer the present to their child "from Mom and Dad" or agree beforehand to give separate gifts that possibly complement each other. For example, the mother buys the skateboard and the father buys the protective gear, or he buys the child an iPod and she buys the iTunes. This way each present is enhanced by the other, eliminating parental competition.

"Should divorced parents continue to give presents to their children 'from Mom and Dad' even after one of the parents remarries?"

Divorced parents who are newly married may not be able to approach joint gift giving easily. The new partner may resent the presentation of his or her new spouse in a couple with the ex. However, if divorced parents share custody or otherwise actively co-parent, it is their responsibility to coordinate efforts with each other. That doesn't mean you exclude the bonusparent, however. Ideally, the gift can be offered "from Mom, Dad, and Jann," for example.

Establishing Clear Boundaries

"My husband's nine-year-old daughter's birthday is this weekend, and she has decided she'd like to go to a movie with girlfriends. My husband and his ex-wife are taking them. Is this appropriate?"

Not really. Once a divorced parent remarries, the new partner becomes the parent's primary companion. In this case, that means that the husband and his ex continue to co-parent but integrate his wife into the mix. Ideally, then, the husband, his ex, and his wife would take the kids to the movies for the bonusdaughter's birthday.

If divorced parents cannot comfortably interact after one has remarried, then the best choice would be to have two separate parties—one hosted by Mom and one hosted by Dad and his new wife. Rarely after a divorced parent remarries should the divorced parents socialize alone with their children.

When a parenting plan works, new spouses are often intimidated by the parents' comfortable interaction and view the ex-couple's casual behavior as inappropriate and possibly even an indicator that they secretly desire reconciliation. This prompts jealousy, insecurity, and a host of bad feelings that are difficult for the new partner to overcome. If the divorced parent feels that stress and therefore wants to attend social situations without the new partner, this only makes the new partner feel *more* insecure.

If a new partner is feeling insecure in the face of the partner's interaction with the ex, it's an indicator that clear boundaries have not been established between the ex-couple. Former spouses must have a clear understanding of how they will interact after the breakup *before* new partners are introduced. And new couples must have a clear understanding about what each expects from the other *before* they marry or move in together.

These types of conversations are not easy and can be uncomfortable, but without them it is impossible to coordinate family events—particularly events such as birthday parties, when all the adults are expected to attend and make the day as fun and memorable as they can.

Turning Rude Party Behavior into Something Positive

Biological parents who face feelings of insecurity and jealousy toward their ex's new partner or spouse can exhibit rude behavior, such as inviting their ex to their child's birthday party while demanding that the ex's new partner not attend. The new partner can respond to such a slight gracefully. Using the 1-2-3 approach, the first step to positive interaction with a partner's ex could be to send the ex an e-mail. Level 2 might be a phone call. Start the communication with something like "I know you don't feel comfortable when I am around, and I regret that. I would just stay home, because I don't want anyone to feel uncomfortable, especially your son. One thing I know we both can agree on is that Jason is wonderful, and I want you to know that I attribute that in part to your influence. If you honestly feel it will make Jason uncomfortable if I attend, then I will talk to Sam and explain why you don't feel it's a good idea that I be there, but right now I'm sort of stuck in the middle of the two of you."

End this part of your conversation with this really important question: "Isn't there a way we can work this out so your son has the great sixth-birthday party he really deserves?" Here's why the question is so important. It forces the person who really has the problem to arrive at an answer. It doesn't point out right or wrong, and it refocuses the emphasis back on the best interests of the child.

Then let her talk, because she will. Bite your tongue and listen. If she's insulting, don't let it get to you. Just end the conversation politely and try again another time. If you are co-parenting, there will always be another opportunity to present your case.

Here's an important tip about the words to use when talking to an ex's new partner. Do not refer to your husband or wife as "my husband" or "my wife" during your first conversations. Until you can communicate easily, call him or her by the first name—in this case "Sam." Saying something like "But my husband wants me to go" will be perceived as rubbing salt in the wound. He used to be *her* husband not so long ago. If you read through the suggested conversation, you will note that the child was first referred to as "your son." That was done on purpose. By using "your son" you are acknowledging the importance of the biological parent. Many exes are secretly concerned that the new partner is trying to usurp their place as father or mother, especially if the new partner does not have children. By referring to the child as "your son" you are telling the biological parent up front that you know your place in regard to the child.

I know these seem like small things, but through my own experiences, and after years of working with first and second spouses, I've learned that it's the words chosen that often prevent or foster good communication.

It is also important to note that most very young children don't really care who comes to their birthday party and don't understand all the grown-up drama behind the divorce and remarriage. When it comes to birthday parties, young kids think, "The more the merrier! More presents for me!"

When a Parent Forgets a Child's Birthday

It's a natural response to want to protect a child who has been hurt. And it is infuriating if an ex whom you perceive as irresponsible and uncaring perpetrates that hurt. But it is particularly important not to transfer your anger and hurt to your child. Empathy is a noble trait, but in this case it may prevent you from being the support your child needs.

If your ex forgets your child's birthday, what your child really needs are some tools to cope with the disappointment. When trying to offer reassurance, remove the negative emotions you feel toward your ex from your interaction with the child. This does not mean you should make excuses or lie for him or her. It means you should look for ways to help your child, not punish your ex.

An appropriate response when your ex has let your child down might be to say something like "Honey, just because we are adults and your parents doesn't mean we have all the answers. We have plenty of things to learn. You are a smart, kind, loving, beautiful person. Remember all the people in your life that you can count on and love you on a daily basis (start naming them together): Grandpa and Grandma, your friends (name some friends specifically). And I love you every minute, and I'm so impressed with (mention something about which you can honestly compliment the child)."

Approaching a child's disillusionment in this manner focuses attention toward the people who really do love and respect the child rather than on the person about whose love the child is uncertain.

Coming-of-Age Celebrations

Coming-of-age ceremonies vary among cultures and religions. They may mark age or religious milestones and are generally a time when family and friends come together for celebration. If family members are divorced or estranged, it can make for a very uncomfortable time—especially for the child. In some cultures, the planning that goes into a coming-of-age ceremony resembles the preparations for a wedding and can be quite elaborate and expensive. Who stands up in the ceremony? Where do estranged family members sit? Who attends the party after the ceremony? If parents and family members cannot work through these questions together, a child's landmark day can easily become just another day of battles. So put your feuds aside and do your best to help the child celebrate his or her special day.

First Communion and Confirmation

Many Catholics are baptized as infants, receive first Communion as children, and are confirmed as adolescents. For the Catholic child, the first Communion usually takes place around the age of six, seven, or eight. It marks the first time a child accepts Communion, or the holy sacrament, and is quite an elaborate church ceremony, sometimes followed by a family celebration. Some Protestant denominations also celebrate the first Communion. The Protestant ceremony is typically less elaborate but may also be followed by a party or family celebration.

Ex-etiquette dictates that divorced parents, family, and friends put their differences aside for this day and help to create a pleasant memory for the child. First Communion attire, along with unanticipated extras for the child, can be quite expensive, and divorced parents should look for a way to split the expenses. In some communities girls wear dresses that have been passed down to them from generation to generation. These dresses are regarded as family heirlooms and should be treated with great respect so that the family tradition can continue even though the parents are divorced.

Confirmation is a religious rite in many Christian churches and is regarded as a public profession of faith prepared for by long and careful religious instruction. Children are usually confirmed at age twelve or thirteen, when, according to the church, they are old enough to choose their faith. In Protestant churches the observance tends to be seen as a rite of passage, similar in some ways to a Jewish child's bar mitzvah or bas mitzvah.

The sacrament of confirmation often takes place in the middle of a mass, so seating is not as critical as during a child's first Communion. A family party is usually held after the confirmation, and the same rules for good behavior between divorced or separated parents and extended family apply here as at a child's first Communion. As with the child's first Communion, divorced parents should consider splitting the cost of special clothing or hosting a family celebration.

"Recently my ex-wife gave me a schedule for our twin daughters' Communion in which my ex and I walk up the aisle together and sit together at the front of the church. My wife feels uncomfortable with this, as do I. How do I stay involved without angering my ex or causing a conflict in my home? Should my wife attend? And, if she does, where does she sit? Should I walk down the aisle with my ex? I can't seem to come up with a plan to make everyone, especially my daughters, comfortable.

The Catholic Church does not recognize divorce, so there really is no formal precedent for the scenario described here—but this is a perfect example of why new rules must be created to match today's lifestyles.

Since the first Communion is performed in a church, civil interaction between divorced parents and their extended families is expected out of respect for the surroundings. To prevent arguments and to set an example for all children attending, special care should be taken to seat battling parents and former family a safe distance apart, perhaps separated by friends or extended-family members. If divorced parents and former family attend the family party following the first Communion, they must all remember to have respect for the host, the host's home, and the children present and leave without incident. Those who feel they cannot remain civil in the presence of an ex at the family get-together should attend the church ceremony and then leave quietly without doing anything that might distract from the importance of the day.

In this case, yes, your new wife should attend the ceremony, especially if your children feel close to her, and she is actively co-parenting with you and your ex. There are a few different ways you can handle the seating at your children's religious milestones.

First, you and your ex should have a formal conversation about how the ceremony should be handled so that there are no surprises at the church. The degree of interaction at the ceremony will depend on how long you have been divorced and how well you and your ex have learned to interact over the years. If this was our family, Sharyl, my husband, and I would walk together, but not all divorced parents would feel comfortable doing so, so that's when you look for alternatives.

The first alternative to all walking together would be that the mother walks the kids down the aisle alone, and the father sits with his wife in the congregation. If the kids balk at this approach, another alternative might be for the dad to wait at the front of the church with the priest while the mom walks the kids down the aisle. Dad greets Mom and the children and then sits next to his wife for the rest of the ceremony. Or Mom might walk alone with the children while Dad sits quietly near the front of the church next to his wife.

If you decide to walk down the aisle with your former wife, as she suggested, it might be best for the twins to walk between the two of you. The message then is that you are both first and foremost their parents, although no longer married, and that you are mutually supportive of your children's religious training. Your wife would then sit with the other family members. If there is a reception afterward, that is when you can make your social statement and be at your new wife's side.

Bar Mitzvahs and Bat Mitzvahs

Bar mitzvahs and bat mitzvahs are coming-of-age ceremonies in which a thirteen-year-old Jewish boy or a twelve-year-old Jewish girl, respectively, reads from the Torah for the first time. During services on the Jewish Sabbath (Saturday), the celebrant is asked to recite blessings and possibly help lead part of the service. A bar or bat mitzvah is a happy family occasion followed by a party celebrating it. Bar mitzvahs and bat mitzvahs are the most important occasions for Jewish children aside from their wedding. Both parents and extended family—regardless of marital status and past disagreements—should attend.

Bar mitzvah and bat mitzvah ceremonies and receptions can be quite elaborate today, rivaling the cost of first weddings and receptions. If the parents of the child are divorced, the planning and financing of the bar mitzvah can be just as complicated as planning a wedding and reception. This is where good ex-etiquette comes into play. If parents divorce before the child comes of age, they should make decisions about the cost of the upcoming bar mitzvah or bat mitzvah at the time of the divorce and include that information in the divorce decree. If they don't do this, then they must agree about the finances at the time of the ceremony. Parents are responsible for the cost of invitations, decorations, food, and reception hall. The most common solution is to split the cost equally.

The wording used for invitations is very similar to that used on a wedding invitation. There is no formal seating arrangement at these ceremonies—no "mother's side" or "father's side" of the synagogue, as with wedding seating. The celebrant is called up to the Torah to recite blessings over the weekly lection. The parents usually sit close to the front of the temple to watch their child and should use common sense if they are estranged. Divorced parents who have remarried sit with their new spouses. If this upsets an ex-spouse, good ex-etiquette says that the ex holds in the discontent, and the remarried couple may sit a distance away to prevent a confrontation that might embarrass the child and other family members. Common gifts include books of religious or educational value, religious items, writing implements, or savings bonds.

The bar mitzvah may also be the time that a young man receives his first tallith, or prayer shawl, which is worn during Jewish religious services. A tallith is likely to be given as a special gift from father to son, teacher to student, or, later in life, from father-in-law to son-in-law. If there is a divorce, a tallith that was given to a son-in-law or other relative by marriage should be treated like any family heirloom and returned to the family of origin, unless there were children produced from the married union. In that case the heirloom may be offered to a child produced from the union before the divorce.

Quinceañera

When a girl reaches her fifteenth birthday in Mexico, Puerto Rico, Cuba, and Central and South America, she celebrates her *quinceañera*, a Latin coming-of-age ceremony. If the family moves to another country, such as the United States, the tradition often follows. The family priest will perform a *quinceañera* ceremony in a church, and the girl's baptismal godparents oversee the spiritual aspects of the celebration.

There is a tricky aspect to ex-etiquette when it comes to the *quinceañera* celebration. Most of the people who live in Mexico,

Puerto Rico, Cuba, and Central and South America are of the Roman Catholic faith and continue to worship as Catholics when they move to another country. Divorce and remarriage are not recognized in the Roman Catholic Church, so parents or other family members who are estranged may not live together but may not be formally divorced either. In these cases, the estranged parents must still co-parent their children. Therefore, the rules of good ex-etiquette still apply and can serve as guidelines for better communication between estranged parents.

The *quinceañera* celebration can be quite expensive and, in fact, is similar to a wedding. The dress worn by the young woman is similar to a wedding dress, and she chooses attendants to support her during her rite of passage. There are flowers and decorations to consider that will match the chosen color scheme for the festivities. A reception is held at which guests are served lunch or dinner, although the party that follows the *quinceañera* is usually more reserved than a wedding reception because the guest of honor is a minor. Often there is dancing and a live band, or a DJ is hired for the evening.

As at a wedding reception, there is a *quinceañera* tradition that the young lady dances the first dance with her father. A special song is chosen, often with Spanish lyrics. A special dance between father and daughter is always a sentimental time, but it is particularly poignant if the parents are estranged. Care should be taken to make this dance as stress-free as possible for the young woman celebrating her *quinceañera*.

Using good ex-etiquette as your guide, the cost of the *quinceañera* should be handled the same way as a wedding that would be held if the parents were estranged. The father usually finances such an affair. Or if the parents have been estranged for years, or the financial situations of the parents lend themselves to it, an agreement is made between the parents about financing.

Adult Birthday Celebrations

Although adults may not anticipate their birthdays with quite as much excitement as kids, it is still a special day that they typically spend surrounded by family and friends. And issues of divorce and remarriage are likely to affect not just the person whose birthday it is but the person hosting the party, extended family, friends, and ex-couples who both were once friends with the celebrant.

Ex-Etiquette for Party Hosts

At Bonus Families the questions we receive about ex-etiquette for adult birthday parties most often come from the host and center on the guest list: "Who should attend?" "Should I invite former family?" "What about friends who seem to have gravitated to the 'other camp'?"

The guest list for an adult's birthday party should include those who are close to the guest of honor—not necessarily those who are close to the host of the party. If you are hosting the party, you must remember to always consider the guest of honor's wishes first. If the guest of honor is friends with both members of a divorced couple, for example, but you are more friendly with the ex-wife, you should not take sides but should invite both of them, notifying each that both they and their ex are invited. Leave up to them the decision about whether or not they attend.

As host you should not expect a guest who is divorced to pass along an invitation or other information to his or her ex, no matter how friendly they may be. No "Gee, I'm sorry I didn't send you an invite. I thought Bill would tell you." And if the divorced couple has a child, the host should never pass on an invitation to either parent through their child.

When You and Your Ex Are Both Invited

Friends often do their best not to take sides after a breakup, and because of this there may be times when ex-spouses are both invited to the same birthday celebration. For example, say you are divorced and your friends are throwing a first-birthday party for their child. Both you and your ex have stayed in contact with the family and have maintained close friendships with them. Now both of you are invited to the same get-together. How do you handle it?

It can be stressful to attend a get-together when you know your ex might be in attendance, but some of this can be alleviated when a good host has notified your ex in advance that you have also been invited. A divorced couple's party conduct should be as cordial as possible, remembering that the primary reason you have been invited is to celebrate with the guest of honor, not to use the party as a vehicle to get back at your ex or make a personal statement of any kind. If you and your ex cannot be cordial with one another in public, you should not attend the party.

At times divorced people ask their host whether or not their ex is planning to attend the party. Their strategy is that if the ex doesn't attend, then they will, or vice versa. This is when hosts hear things like "If she is coming, I'm not!" This is very poor ex-etiquette. It is not the host's responsibility to mediate between exes. The only responsibility a host has to his or her guests is to be gracious, kind, and polite. It is expected that guests will do likewise. However, if you want to attend the party and truly feel that you can be civil but your ex cannot, and so you want to know if he or she will be there, you might have a friend casually ask the host who will be attending. Then make your decision based on that information, and politely accept or decline the invitation without elaborating on the reason.

Inviting Former Family

> "I'm throwing a fortieth-birthday party for my wife, whose first husband passed away. They had a daughter together, who is now fourteen. My wife remains close to her first husband's parents, and I have to admit I have a problem with it. Should I invite my wife's former in-laws to her party?"

This bonusfamily life of combining past and present can be difficult to master. And for many who have been raised with an old-school divorce philosophy, it is an entirely new mind-set.

It makes sense that your wife stays in contact with her former in-laws. She formed a personal bond with them while married to their son. But more important, they are her daughter's grandparents. She is right to stay in contact with her child's extended family and nurture the grandchild-grandparent relationship.

Now, if your wife had *not* had children with her late husband, the answer would not be as clear-cut. It would be understandable if she remained close to her former in-laws after their son's passing, but if there were no children involved, then the relationship might diminish once she remarried.

Hosts who have questions about the guest list or appropriate behavior at a party should simply ask themselves this question: "Who is this party for?" That relieves the host from having to make any personal judgments and to decide without prejudice. In this case, this is a milestone fortieth-birthday party for your wife. You would therefore invite her closet friends—not necessarily the people *you* feel most comfortable with. Her former in-laws probably fall into that category.

To eliminate any embarrassing gossip at the party, put some thought into how you will introduce your wife's former in-laws so that everyone will have something to discuss at ease when they meet. Be as gracious as you can. As much as your wife's relationship with her former in-laws bothers you, remember that the deceased was their child, and your wife's child is their beloved grandchild.

Anniversary Celebrations

Through the years a couple builds a legacy that can't be measured in material possessions but rather in the lives the couple has touched through their union. For couples who have been through divorce and possibly remarriage, anniversaries can mean something different to everyone around them—exes, kids, former family, bonusfamily—and care should be taken to ensure that anniversary celebrations follow the rules of good ex-etiquette.

Former Anniversaries

It is inappropriate for an ex to call attention to his or her former wedding anniversary. Sending e-mails or cards or leaving a message on the answering machine or voice mail asking "Do you know what day it is today?" are all in poor taste. Don't do it. You are divorced, and if your ex has remarried, you must respect the new union.

Some people have told me that wishing their ex a happy anniversary was done as an inside joke meant for the ex, not for his or her new partner—a sort of "remember when" chuckle. This is still not good ex-etiquette. If you have been attempting to cultivate trust with your ex's new partner—perhaps because you co-parent children—and the new partner finds out about the "joke," it will undermine all the work you have done. Find another joke *that will make the couple laugh*. That will ensure your place as co-parent far better than a furtive wink.

Extended-family members and children of the previously married couple should also not call attention to a past anniversary, unless their relative is a widow or widower and they are paying their respects to the now-ended marital union.

Young children often ask their divorced parents the date of their parents' wedding. This is understandable. Children who ask such questions are probably searching for their roots, some proof that their parents were at one time happy, and assurance that their birth was not a mistake. However, discussing the wedding date and happy beginning of your former marriage should be done with care. It can muster conflicted feelings in a child, possibly undermining the child's relationship with the bonusparent. I have found that the best way to discuss the date of a former marriage with children is to offer the date when asked while explaining that even though that marriage is over, and Daddy or Mommy has remarried, their love for the child is intact and always will be.

Anniversary Milestones

Whether you're celebrating your fifth, tenth, twenty-fifth, or fiftieth anniversary (because I am often asked: couples who divorce and then later remarry each other may celebrate the anniversary of the date of their *first* wedding, counting the years from that date), the longer you have been married, the more time there has been for the relationships around you to change. With those changes come struggles with allegiance and betrayal to past and present family members.

"We are planning our fiftieth-wedding anniversary and would like to invite my brother's ex-wife, who has been in our life for thirty years. He has been divorced for eight years and remarried for six, and he feels that our inviting his ex would be disrespectful to him and his new wife. Over the years we have tried to keep our interactions separate, but for this celebration, it just won't work. He has adult children from his first marriage who will be attending and would like their mother there. Would this be inappropriate for us to do?"

No, it would not be inappropriate in this particular case. Maintaining a relationship with a former relative is your decision and really should not come into question unless he or she blatantly betrayed or publicly humiliated your family member in some way. Then, if you disregarded your brother's request, I would question your judgment. However, if there was no betrayal, then your brother must understand that over the years you have built a friendship with his ex that is separate from his relationship with her. In addition, you might remind him that this woman whom he does not want you to invite is the mother of your nieces and nephews, who will be in attendance. You are aunt to her children. Her absence at this sort of family gathering would be conspicuous at best.

Guests should not attempt to influence a party's guest list. As much as it may infuriate your brother and his new wife, the fact that he and your former sister-in-law had children together secured your former sister-in-law's position in the family. It would not be appropriate for her to attend every family gathering, but for something this special it is quite fitting. Everyone should remain cordial and pay their respects, and those who find staying too uncomfortable can quietly leave without bringing attention to their departure.

It's your fiftieth anniversary—a milestone very few couples reach. When your brother has been married for fifty years, he can invite whomever he likes. This time, for your sake, his current wife and he must be more gracious.

Family Reunions

A typical family reunion assembles as many relatives as can be found for a meal, some recreation, and good times. Such occasions are a great opportunity to update family records and perpetuate extended-family relationships. Attending a family reunion when you know an ex will be there, however, can be a little like walking into the feud between the Hatfields and the McCoys. Just coordinating the logistics of a big reunion is difficult enough. Add in age-old rivalries, hot-blooded differences of opinion, and unresolved divorces, and you have the makings of one particularly volatile family celebration if good ex-etiquette is not observed.

> *"I have been divorced for twenty years. I have never remarried, and my kids are grown. My daughter came home from college last night with an invitation to a family reunion from her father's side of the family. I have not talked to any of them since the divorce, but my daughter wants me to go. Her father has recently separated from his wife, and I think my daughter is entertaining the notion that we might reconcile. There is no chance of that, but there are some former relatives whom I would like to see. What is proper ex-etiquette in regard to ex-family reunions?"*

Approach a family reunion just like any other family get-together that former family might attend. If you have not received a direct invitation, you really should not attend. If you do choose to go, however, perhaps as your daughter's escort, remain cordial and polite and do not make a scene. Remember, it's a *family* reunion, so children will be present.

Another circumstance here is important to address. Children often harbor a secret desire for their parents to reconcile—even after twenty years apart. In my work I have come to see that this can be a very real wish for young children. On growing into adulthood, children may recognize that reconciliation is improbable but instead are looking for proof of some sort of connection between the parents that brought them into the world. Even if the connection is merely an acceptance that together they made a child, the acknowledgment makes the difference. If the divorced parents present their past relationship as a mistake, then the children internalize that to feel as if *they* were a mistake. Knowing this, avoid saying things like "I will always love your father. We just couldn't live together" because adult children quickly see through that gobbledygook. Something like "Your father and I will always have a common bond—and that bond is our mutual love for you" acknowledges the parents' past relationship—plus the parent-child relationship in the past, present, and future.

Class Reunions

Class reunions can be especially difficult for people who are divorced. When you are disappointed by your dating prospects after divorce, and there's a class reunion on the horizon, that's when you might find yourself pining for your past love from high school or college. Be careful. The likelihood is slim that the romanticized version you have kept in your head over the years is exactly what you will see when you stand face-to-face with that old flame. Good reunion ex-etiquette suggests that you are honest when seeing your ex. Do your best not to embellish or out and out lie about what you have accomplished during the time that has passed. If a current partner accompanies your ex, do not openly reminisce about your first time together. No dirty dancing as the new partner looks on. No secret trysts in the bathroom. Be respectful of their union. They may have children, and the last thing you want to do is cause problems between parents.

All that said, if you and a former girlfriend or boyfriend are both single at the time of the reunion, and there's chemistry between you, then no holds are barred. I first met my husband when he was thirteen years old. I am of the mind that people's basic moral codes are established when they are very young. If they were nice in high school, they are probably nice now. My husband and I married twenty-one years later, a few years shy of our twentieth high school reunion. Since we were quite good friends in high school, going to our reunion twenty years later as husband and wife had quite a few heads turning.

Giving Toasts

Many gatherings and parties require toasts at some point during the festivities. A toast that refers to an ex when the present partner is in attendance is rude and very bad ex-etiquette. It makes the new partner uncomfortable and the guests as well. Even comments that seem insignificant can be of concern. For example, I recently attended a fortieth-birthday party of a friend. It was hosted by his fiancée. Another old friend began the festivities with a toast that talked about how long they had known each other. He began his tribute with "I met John years ago when he was married to his first wife, Sue. Sue was quite a good-looking woman in those days, and I was driving down the street and noticed her in her driveway. John was under the car changing a tire. . . ." He then went on to talk about some of the crazy things they had done over the years, which were quite funny, but the mood was already set. Each time he mentioned John's ex, the guests would cringe. A better way to have explained how long they had known each other would have been to say, "I've known John for over twenty years." Then look at John and say, "We've had some good times, haven't we John? I remember one time . . ." But make sure that "one time" did not include John's ex-wife or something that would be embarrassing to his fiancée. Then, at the end of the toast, thank John's fiancée for including you and throwing such a great party.

4

Ex-Etiquette for School Events and Extracurricular Activities

"Let us put our minds together and see what life we can make for our children."

—Sitting Bull

What is good ex-etiquette for a child's first day of school? Should divorced parents attend school conferences together? Who pays for your daughter's expensive prom dress? Where do divorced parents and bonusparents sit at their child's high school graduation? How do you make sure that your child is never uncomfortable or embarrassed in front of classmates or teammates? The many issues concerning children's academic, extracurricular, and social lives after divorce and remarriage can be the most volatile and emotional we face, but they can be faced with confidence if the first rule of good ex-etiquette, to put the children first, is always observed.

Good Ex-Etiquette for School Activities

Children learn not only academics at school but also how to behave socially. Here they meet friends who may be companions for years. Many children see school activities as the most important events in their lives.

When parents are divorced, a child's school activities can also be a source of great irritation. After a breakup parents may not see the advantage of cooperating with each other, and either out of spite or indifference they withhold from one another important dates and times of their child's school activities. Divorced parents may get more and more frustrated with each passing year, until they completely lose sight of their children's best interests. Information becomes a weapon of power, and there is victory in knowing that back-to-school night starts at 7:00 instead of 7:30 P.M.

The First Day of School

For many parents, the first day of school is a mark that their little baby is growing up, and the day can be quite emotional. If a dad and mom have split up, the first day of school, rather than being a landmark day for the child, can become just something else the divorced parents argue about.

> *"My little girl is scheduled to be with me for her first day of school, and I do not think her mother should be present when I drop her off at her new classroom!"*

Some children, especially those with older siblings, may look forward to this big day, while others may be fearful of the change from the smaller and more relaxed preschool environment. So ask yourself, "How can I best help my child cope with this day?" If it's having both parents there to drop her off, then make that decision. If that is not in the child's best interest, your ex should be willing to accept that decision. Your ex should not force the issue that both parents attend if you cannot present a united front for the sake of your child. Stressed-out parents cannot calm a stressed-out child.

Here's a suggested compromise. The child is scheduled to be with you for the first day of school. Her mom would like to participate, but you are a stickler about adhering to the parenting plan and do not want your ex to accompany your daughter and you on the first day. A few days before school starts, you might suggest that she take your daughter to meet her teacher and get familiar with the new school and classroom. You can then drop the child off the first day, chat with the teacher, and pick up your daughter after school. Another possibility is for you to bring along a camera to take some candid first-day-of-school pictures in the child's classroom and give them to her mom. The key is to look for the compromise that will offer the child the most security at what could be a very stressful time.

Saying good-bye when dropping off your child for the first day of school can be an emotional time for both child and parent. To set a positive stage, try to send your child off with a smile and a wave along with the reassurance that Mommy, Daddy, or someone familiar will be there to pick them up later.

Parent-Teacher Conferences and Back-to-School Nights

Parent-teacher conferences and back-to-school nights are a true bone of contention for both biological and bonusparents. Biological parents often resent a stepparent's interest in attending their child's school conference, feeling that the stepparent is crossing the line into their territory. Bonusparents who help co-parent their partner's children may feel it's their responsibility to attend their bonuschild's school activities. It's a difficult line to walk, and both positions are understandable.

Rather than use parent-teacher conferences or back-to-school nights as just another reason to feel threatened, biological and bonusparents can best serve the children in their care by truly examining how they can work together in the best interest of the child. Nothing is more distracting to a child's ability to learn than to be shuffled between two homes with parents who are constantly at odds.

The first year after I married Sharyl's ex, she and I interacted only when necessary. When school conferences rolled around, Sharyl went to one, and Larry and I went to another. We compared notes afterward, but it was apparent that we did not hear the same things from the teacher, and homework, permission slips, and sports equipment continued to get misplaced or overlooked. Out of frustration, the next year we all attended the same conference, which the teacher was not expecting! She was quite flustered when, after about three minutes of meeting with Sharyl, Larry and I walked in and sat down. Make sure the teacher expects that both parents and their new partners will attend the same conference. This will allow the teacher to prepare by having two of everything ready to go back to both homes.

Tips to Make Parent-Teacher Conferences More Productive

- If a child's time is divided between the parental homes, living some of the time with one parent and some with the other, make sure that a representative from each home is present at the conference. This ensures that there are no misunderstandings between homes. Ideally, the representatives should be the biological parents. New partners need not attend conferences unless they contribute to the caregiving of the children. (I always attended the kids' conferences because I was the primary caregiver when they lived in my home.)

- Ask questions. Come to the conference with a list of questions regarding your child's academic and social issues as well as questions about the teacher's philosophy. Some good questions to ask include:

  ⇨ What can we do from both homes to support our child's learning?

  ⇨ How can both homes help our child to excel? What can both homes do to prevent our child from falling behind?

  ⇨ What are our child's strongest and weakest subjects?

  ⇨ How well does our child get along with classmates?

- Share information about your child with teachers and co-parents. Teachers need your help as they educate your children. Explain your child's living situation, that he or she has two homes, and introduce all the parent figures if possible. Ask for two of everything, from homework worksheets to permission slips. Discuss homework rules at both homes. The more you share about your child, the better the teacher will be able to meet the child's needs.

- Raise issues of concern. Biological and bonusparents should agree ahead of time about the issues they want to discuss with the teacher. Do not use your child's parent-teacher conference as a counseling session or as a place to point fingers or blame the other parent. When expressing concerns, be tactful. Take note of what the teacher has to say in response to a problem. Then put a plan in place to find a solution together.

- Take notes during the conference so that you remember everything and can keep anyone who was unable to attend the conference informed. After the meeting, review your notes. If something is unclear, schedule a follow-up meeting with the teacher to clarify.

Tips to Make Back-to-School Night Run Smoothly

If parents cannot act civilly in public, do not embarrass your child by attending back-to-school night at the same time. Make an agreement for one to go at the beginning of the night and the other toward the end of the night.

- Do not hoard your child's work or hide it from the other parent. Either delegate one parent to save the child's work for posterity or be sensitive to each other and share your child's successes.
- Introduce yourself to the teachers and teachers' aides. Make sure that they know all the players—Mom and Dad and any new partners—and that they have up-to-date phone numbers and e-mail addresses for all parent figures.
- Make sure the teacher is willing to supply two of everything handed out at back-to-school night—one for Mom and one for Dad.
- Make it a point to congratulate your child for doing good work, and share how proud you are of the child's accomplishments.

Proms and Dances

"My daughter wants to go to her junior prom, but I can't afford the formal dress she wants. I told her to ask her dad for help, and she did, but I just got a raging phone call from an angry ex

telling me what a witch I am for making him look bad. What did I do wrong? The dress is expensive, and I really can't afford it!"

Although your motives may be genuine, let's look at what the "Go ask your dad" comment is really saying. If the father can't afford the dress either, who ends up looking like the bad guy? Her father, because he was the last person to say no. That's why he was angry. He was unwittingly set up to look like the bad guy in front of his daughter.

What should have been done? Don't tell children to ask their other parent for something. Put them on hold, along the lines of "I'll figure something out." Then call the other parent, explain the situation, and together look for a solution to the problem. A perfectly acceptable solution could be to split the cost of the prom dress. Your daughter gets the dress, no one looks like the bad guy, and you and your ex have laid a positive groundwork for working together in the future.

School Plays, Sports, and Other School-Related Events

Divorced parents should approach their children's events in the same manner—you are both attending in the best interest of your child. Ideally, both parents should attend their child's plays, concerts, or sporting events. It is not necessary to sit together, but it is necessary for the child to know that both of you are there. Your goal is to be cordial in public, but if your relationship is tempestuous, the best course of action is for you to sit in separate areas so that you will not cause a scene. Both of you are there to support the child, not to establish territory or make a statement about your love lives.

Refrain from any behavior that would cause the child embarrassment. Certainly avoid confronting your ex or your ex's new partner while your child, his friends, or other parents look on. To achieve this, conversations between estranged parents should be kept to a minimum while attending children's events—no arguing in the parking lot after a soccer game, for example. That is the quickest way to ostracize children and expose them to gossip, not to mention making them dread their future milestone events. If there is something that you feel must be discussed with your ex, make an appointment to discuss it privately at another time.

If one parent cannot attend a performance or event, the attending parent should do everything possible to not undermine the absent parent—even if that parent has been continually flaky. A child always knows when a parent is irresponsible. It will not make the child feel more secure or happier about his or her performance to have one parent drive home the other parent's poor parenting. This is the time to concentrate only on how well the child has performed. Finally, you should never under any circumstance become so blinded by your drama with your ex that you leave your child's extracurricular activity without first acknowledging it and saying "Good job!"

"I recently went to my son's school play. Eric had a great part— the singing bunny. I got there late and the lights were already dim, so I could barely see. I did notice my ex and tried to sit nearby. When the lights came up during intermission, I found myself sitting next to my ex's new in-laws. It was very uncomfortable, and I didn't know what to say. How should I have handled this situation?"

First, in the future, do the best you can to be on time at your child's activities. He may not be able to fully relax until you are there, and it will help him to know where you are sitting before the play or concert starts.

Second, understand that your ex's new in-laws will now be part of your child's—and thus your—life. The more comfortable you act around them, the more comfortable your son will be. Be calm and simply introduce yourself: "Hello, I'm Don Collins, Eric's father." Or if you want to break the ice with a little levity, try "Hello, I'm Don Collins, the singing bunny's father." You may be wondering what you can possibly talk about until the play resumes. Your common ground is your mutual interest—in this case the singing bunny.

Facing the "Other Woman" or "Other Man"

"I am having a very hard time being cordial to my ex and his new wife. He left me for her, and within a year they were married. Now they both show up at my kids' soccer games. Is it asking too much for him to stay away on my days with the kids? I don't want to see either of them. What is good ex-etiquette in these types of situations?"

You start your speech like t his: "I would like to thank the Academy . . ." because when your child is around, you will have to perfect your acting skills. The truth is, there is no more difficult situation than the one you describe here. All the emotions you undoubtedly feel—anger, frustration, betrayal—are understandable, but actively responding to how you feel will not make your child feel more secure, which is your main priority.

I'm not suggesting that you don't acknowledge your own pain. Grieving is a very important part of starting over. However, when a breakup and the pain of betrayal are very new, to prevent public outbursts you might suggest to your ex that you take turns watching the children's games, plays, or other extracurricular activities. It will not always be this way. There will be a time when you must all appear in public for a special occasion. With any luck, you will be able to face it with grace and dignity. If you act politely in public, it doesn't mean you are condoning your ex's betrayal; it is just the measure of the type of person you are and how much you love your child.

It should be said that it was very insensitive to both you and the children for your former spouse to show up so soon at the children's activities with his new love interest. Whether the new partner was the cause of the separation or not, it was just too soon to introduce a new partner into the scenario. It would have been better to let the children get used to the idea that their parents were no longer together, make sure the divorce was final, then slowly introduce the new love interest with as much sensitivity as possible. This doesn't really help the ex who doesn't *ever* want to be confronted by his or her ex's current date. But if it has been a while since the separation, the divorce is final, and your ex has remarried, there's not much you can do to stop the kids' new bonusparent from going to the children's extracurricular activities. At this point, the new bonusparent is trying to be supportive, and it is in the children's best interest that he or she is involved.

The best revenge for parents who have been betrayed by their child's other parent is to pull their life together and make a success out of the future. So here's the 1-2-3 approach to good ex-etiquette in this situation.

Level 1: The parents are so angry that they can't be in each other's presence without arguing in front of the kids. Therefore, only one parent at a time goes to the game.

Level 2: The divorced parents do not necessarily like to interact, but they understand that they must, to support their child. They both attend the game but sit far away from each other. I must point out, however, that sometimes this is even more stressful for the child than if the estranged parents take turns attending the games. It can be difficult for children to concentrate when they know their parents are so angry with each other that they must sit a soccer field apart when watching a game. At one of my own children's Little League games I witnessed divorced parents sitting on different sides of the bleachers. When their child hit a home run he had no idea where to look first for reinforcement. His eyes went to his mom in the stands as he ran, then to his dad on the other side of the field. He was clearly distraught. With this in mind, if you can't sit together, try just a few rows apart. Standing an entire soccer field away from each other only advertises to everyone your inability to put your child first.

Level 3: Both parents understand the importance of presenting a united front for their child despite their breakup. They sit in the same vicinity while watching the game. The child knows exactly where to look to get positive reinforcement when hitting a home run or kicking a goal. The family has reached bonus status and collaborate in the best interest of the child.

Who Brings the Snack? . . . and Other Petty Disputes

"This upcoming weekend is my ex's weekend with the kids. I have custody; he has visitation. It's our son's turn to take snacks to his soccer game on Saturday. My ex has insisted that I agree not to attend any soccer game that falls on his weekend and has demanded his 'fair share' of soccer practices. Therefore, is it my responsibility or his responsibility to provide snacks for soccer?"

It sounds as if both parents have lost track of what is important. Let me take a stab at what might be going on here. Very often parents in your position secretly feel that, because they were granted custody, *they* are the true parent, and the other parent is merely babysitting on the visitation weekend. The noncustodial parent, resentful and bitter, becomes uncooperative, which many noncustodial parents feel is the only ammunition they have to get back at the ex for gaining custody of "my" child. The custodial parent in return gets angry and bitter and becomes uncooperative. As a result, you have two uncooperative parents fighting over little things like whose responsibility it is to bring snacks.

You said that your ex wants his "fair share" of games and practices, implying that he doesn't want anyone to impose on "his time" with his child. Even though Dad seems to be the culprit here, you may be contributing to the problem without even knowing it. Whose soccer games are these anyway? They aren't Mom's games, and they aren't Dad's games. It's not "Mom's time" or "Dad's time." They are your child's soccer games, and it's your child's time. Shouldn't you both be supporting your child as best you can *all the time* and *at every game*?

I suggest that, as the custodial parent, you supply snacks and use them as a gesture to help start a dialogue about how to handle such issues in the future. Can't talk to your ex? Try asking for his suggestions. You don't have to take them to heart, but the act of asking often starts both parties on the road to compromise and better communication—which is what both of you need. Neither of you is in this alone.

Sharing Trophies and Awards

Believe it or not, divorced parents and their new partners commonly battle over their children's Little League trophies or Student of the Month awards. This is what happens when parents allow themselves to get caught up in a personal vendetta and lose sight of what is in the best interest of the children. The trophies are not the parent's trophies. The trophies reward the child for participation in Little League—not the parent's involvement in Little League. The Student of the Month award marks the child's accomplishments, not the parent's accomplishments.

The easiest solution is to agree to designate one parent to store the trophies and other trinkets. But if a child has a bedroom at both parents' homes, and both parents would like to display their child's trophies, simply arrange for two trophies to be conferred. When the coach asks for money to buy your child's trophy, pay for two. The same applies if a special award is presented to your child at school. Ask the teacher or principal to make two awards. Incredibly simple, I know. This is coming from a bonusmom who has hoarded her share of trophies.

Graduation Ceremonies and Parties

Every year, as June approaches, I start to get e-mails and phone calls from divorced parents about the proper way to handle their child's graduation. They tend to find all sorts of reasons why they should not attend their child's graduation if their ex is planning to show up. And it gets worse if the ex has even hinted at bringing someone new along.

Let's get right to the point: offering ultimatums and putting pressure on your child based on the fact that the other parent will be in attendance at any special occasion, but most of all, a special occasion that celebrates the child's achievements, is extremely poor ex-etiquette. As with other family events and celebrations, divorced parents and extended family should exhibit cordial behavior toward one another at graduation exercises. If divorced parents are at odds, they do not have to sit in the same vicinity, but both parents should attend, and the child should know exactly where each of them is sitting. If one parent has remarried or has a partner, that person should also be there. It should be understood that a parent's new partner's attendance at a graduation ceremony is not meant to insult the ex but to support the child. It should also be noted that graduations and other "family" celebrations are not times to introduce casual dates to the family. A parent who does not have a significant other at the time should go alone or with an extended-family member who also cares about the child. Good ex-etiquette for graduations reinforces the obvious—the more positive support the young person gets, the better.

As for graduation parties, the custodial parent usually holds the party and does most of the planning, although the responsibility for planning may be split between the two parents if they like. The non-custodial parent should offer to help pay for the party and may also suggest guests from his or her side of the family whose presence would be agreeable to the graduate.

If the parents of the graduate are estranged, then having two separate parties is an alternative. One parent throwing a party and the other hosting a dinner or luncheon on a different date is another option. If two separate parties is the choice, some amount of coordination between the divorced parents—even if estranged—is essential to ensure that both do not plan to have their party on the same day.

If there are other estranged family members in addition to the parents, perhaps as the result of a family rift, other arrangements should be made with the graduate. Do not attempt to make amends at a family get-together, especially one that is a milestone for a child.

"My wife and I both have a kid graduating from high school this year—my son from my first marriage and her daughter from hers. Do we have one party for both of them, or should we plan two separate parties?"

That really depends on your family dynamic and how well you have merged into a family unit. Your children could possibly feel slighted by one party, or they could see it as a time for a huge celebration. It's not uncommon for the parents of good friends to throw one party for a group of friends, so bonussiblings don't necessarily have to feel slighted by this approach. But it is best to have an open conversation and ask for the graduates' honest feelings. If the graduates are leaning toward separate parties, however, it is important to point out that many of the same people would be invited to both parties, and it could be embarrassing to both them and you to invite the same people to the same home for the same reason on two separate days. A better alternative is to plan a joint celebration but to look for ways to help each graduate stand out as an individual: two cakes, for example, and separate toasts with a discussion of their individual accomplishments. Never compare them. Reinforce their individuality, and don't forget to look to the graduates for suggestions. They may opt for another alternative altogether—a trip or a spectacular graduation gift.

The key is cooperation—on the part of the divorced parents and extended family and on the part of the graduates. If the children have been brought up in a spirit of compromise and fairness, they will use these tools to find a solution to the problem. If they have been brought up by battling parents and extended family who rarely talk and hold grudges, they will most likely resort to using those tools instead.

.

5

Ex-Etiquette at Times of Loss and Grieving

"When you teach your son, you teach your son's son."

—The Talmud

The sadness we feel when someone we know passes can be overwhelming. Couple our sadness with the bitterness of divorce, and the feeling of loss and personal grief are compounded. That may be why so many questions arise for divorced couples about how to handle different aspects of funeral arrangements—from wondering whether you should attend your ex's funeral to the appropriate condolences to send to former family. Most people find themselves confused about how to act when someone passes away after divorce has affected the relationship, whether it is an ex-spouse, a divorced friend, or an ex-relative.

When There Has Been a Grudge

In the ten years that I have been a divorce and stepfamily mediator, I have never once met anyone who claimed to be proud of having the ability to hold a grudge. I have only seen it cause families pain and regret—especially when someone dies. Grudges held in the wake of divorce affect everyone—not just the ex-couple but also other relationships with family members and friends, creating vendettas that can go on for generations. When you hold a grudge, ask yourself whether your ability to hold a grudge or your ability to forgive is the legacy you want to pass on through your family. That is the reason for ex-etiquette rule number six, "Don't hold grudges"—to head off facing the consequences when someone has passed and it is too late for resolution.

Attending the funeral of someone against whom you have held a grudge can be appropriate. It can be a demonstration of forgiveness and might also set the stage for healing if family members took sides after the initial disagreement.

Sending Condolences

When an ex passes, sending a note of condolence to his or her current spouse or to your former family will most likely be a welcome gesture, even if the relationship has been strained. Good ex-etiquette suggests that you do not make explicit references to your relationship with your ex in your card. Don't say, for example, "I remember when

Bill and I were very young and we discussed what it would be like should one of us pass." That would not be comforting to the present spouse, who has just lost her husband. Also to be avoided is gushing about what a wonderful person the ex was. A current wife who receives a card saying "Bill was such a wonderful, sweet guy" may be concerned that you have pined for her husband all these years, and that would make future interaction (should you both have Bill's children) uncomfortable.

Some people might think I'm paying too much attention to the exact wording of a condolence note. However, when people are grieving, their emotions run high, and something quite innocent may be misunderstood. It's better to stick with something like "I am very sorry for your loss. Bill will surely be missed." And sign the card "Sincerely."

Who Attends the Funeral?

Although discretion and common sense are always the best guides to proper funeral ex-etiquette, a few other principles apply. If relations between them were cordial, then it is appropriate for a divorced person to attend the funeral of his or her ex. It is also appropriate to attend the funeral of your ex's relation, providing you were close to the deceased, and especially if that relationship was maintained after the divorce. A brief visit to the funeral home is also appropriate. If a funeral is private, however, then friends should not attend unless expressly asked. This would include ex-spouses who are on cordial terms with the family. No matter how well you get along, do not assume you are regarded as family. Wait for a sign from the family that they would like you to be included.

When attending a memorial service or funeral, an ex should not try to join the bereaved family unless formally invited to do so. In such situations, former spouses should do their best not to call attention to themselves. If you catch the eye of a family member who looks interested in engaging in conversation, a sincere smile or possibly a hug is good medicine for anyone who is hurting, but move on quickly.

If your ex remarried, and there has been bitterness between you and the present spouse, it may be more advisable for you to send flowers and a note expressing sympathy than to attend the funeral. Find a way to be supportive no matter what went on in the past. If your presence would be more disruptive than comforting, it is best for you to stay away.

Making Amends

Attending a funeral and offering your sympathies is a sign of respect for the person who passed away as well as for the remaining relatives. It is also an excellent way to set the stage for better relations in the future. Funerals are *not*, however, the proper place to try to make amends. In fact, any special occasion when it's someone else's day— a wedding, graduation, birthday party, or funeral—is not a day to make your first attempt at making amends with someone. Waiting for Uncle Bill's funeral or Lisa's graduation before you extend an olive branch is not good ex-etiquette. Do it *before* the special day so that when you see each other you can both support the person whose day it really is.

On a personal note, my mother passed suddenly years ago, and I vividly remember the note I received from my ex-husband. Although we were cordial because of co-parenting our daughter, conversation did not always come easily. In his note he expressed his deep sorrow and his affection for my mother, plus offered his assistance in any way. It was a lovely sentiment and was appreciated by my entire family. Don't discount the fact that the death of a loved one can break down previous barriers and put many issues into their proper perspective. And when the propriety of an ex-spouse's attendance at a funeral is in question, the children can be the best barometer. Although I had remarried, and my daughter had formed a loving bond with her bonusfather, there was nothing like having her daddy next to her in her time of grief after her grandmother's passing. My ex-husband's kind words and loving presence at my mother's funeral enabled everyone to interact more easily in the future.

Here's another personal story. After a long illness, my husband's mother asked to pass at home. Sharyl had remained close to my husband's parents after she and my husband divorced, but she was quick to allow our family private time in the days before my mother-in-law's death. When it looked as if the time was drawing near, she sent a message asking if she could pay her respects to her former mother-in-law. Asking in this manner made it very easy for us to either invite her or to graciously decline her request without embarrassment. I was taking care of my mother-in-law at that time and was with her almost every day. I will never forget how her face lit up when Sharyl walked into her bedroom. There were no thoughts of her son's divorce or Sharyl's being an "ex," just genuine affection for the mother of her grandchildren. Days later, we called Sharyl and asked her to join us at my mother-in-law's home. Her children were there, and although my husband and I were there to comfort them, I could tell that they wanted their mother there, too. When Grandma passed, we were all with her, including Sharyl.

Funeral Seating

Just as at a wedding ceremony, the first few rows of seating at a funeral service are reserved for the immediate family. In general, exes should sit in the back of the church to pay respects. If one member of a divorced couple with children dies, then the remaining parent should sit with the children at the funeral, unless the remaining parent was estranged from the deceased parent and children; then the children should sit with the relative or close friend with whom they will live.

If a child of a divorced couple passes, the mother usually sits in the front row, alone or with her escort and possibly her other children. The father and his partner may also sit in the front row if everyone gets along. If there are no additional children, and everyone sits in the front, you may want to use other relatives as a buffer between the bereaved mom and dad and their partners. If the divorced parents cannot get along, or there is bad blood between past and present spouses, Dad usually sits next to his significant other in the second row, behind his ex-wife. If this is still a little too close for comfort, use grandparents or other relatives as a buffer in the second row, while he and his wife sit in the third row.

It is inappropriate to relegate a stepparent or a new partner to the back of the room during a funeral ceremony. A stepparent or partner who has a long and established relationship with the family should unquestionably sit with his or her spouse or partner. If there are extenuating circumstances—say an affair broke up the marriage only a short time before the funeral, and those in mourning are still reeling from the whole thing—then it is inappropriate for the new partner to attend at all.

"My ex-husband's sister just lost her son. She and I were good friends during my marriage to her brother, but I've only spoken to her once since my divorce five years ago. Both my ex and I have remarried. I would like to pay my respects, and I'm wondering whether it would be completely out of place if my new husband and I attended the funeral. Besides, enough time has gone by now, and I'd like to be there for my ex. Should we go to the funeral?"

That all depends. If you are going as a friend, to add your support at the loss of your friend's son, then going to the funeral would be a good way to let your old friend know you haven't forgotten her. It's only natural that you would want to bring your husband along for support. However, this is also a former family member, and given that you have not spoken in years because of your divorce, showing up with a new husband might be construed as a slap in the face to that side of the family and completely inappropriate in a time of mourning.

Tragedies like this are sometimes the catalyst for resolving past conflicts, but the funeral is not the proper place to resolve them. Under the circumstances, a heartfelt card with expressions of sympathy may be all that's needed to let your ex-sister-in-law know that you are sorry for her loss. In the card you might tell her how often you think of her and how much you wish that there was some way you could both put the past behind you. If the former family member sees it that way, she will give you a call to thank you for your kind thoughts.

Note that there is no mention of your ex-husband in my response. That is because both of you have remarried. Although it is important for former partners to remain cordial for their children's sake, it is not an ex's place to "support" an ex when the ex has remarried. It is his new partner's responsibility—and privilege, for that matter. If you feel like some communication with him is necessary, again, a note is appropriate.

Obituaries

An obituary is a short but very important overview of someone's life and accomplishments that is published after they have died in the newspaper or other media. It usually lists events or accomplishments in chronological order and includes the deceased's birthplace and birth date, parents' names, schools, jobs, military service, places of residence, affiliations and volunteer activities, and retirement information. Living family members should be listed in the following order:

spouse, children, grandchildren and great-grandchildren, parents, grandparents, siblings, aunts and uncles, cousins, nieces and nephews, common-law spouse, fiancé or fiancée or other companion. Stepchildren and stepgrandchildren, stepparents, and stepsiblings should be fully identified and listed immediately after biological children, grandchildren, parents, or siblings. Ex-spouses should be listed in a separate paragraph if the family so wishes. Deceased spouses, children, and parents may also be named. Other deceased relatives need not be included.

> *"My husband just died and everyone is very upset. He raised my teenaged son since my son was three, and I know that, in addition to his biological kids' names, my husband would want my son's name added to the list after the words 'and loving father of . . .' in the newspaper announcement. But my husband's children do not want my son's name included. What is good ex-etiquette?"*

It sounds as though your son had a good relationship with your late husband, and so he may also feel that being referred to as "son" in the paper is a fitting tribute to the man who raised him. By the same token, the biological children, who also hold their dad in high regard, wish to be singled out in tribute to their father.

The problem here lies in the fact that your deceased husband, your son, and you, for that matter, probably did not view this father-son relationship as a "step" relationship. When most people think of a step relation, they think of someone who is not as close as blood relatives. But your husband raised your son, and they formed a close bond (the very reason we have abandoned the "step" terminology and have adopted "bonus"). Because you imply that your son and your husband each viewed the other as a bonus to their lives, the newspaper announcement could read:

" . . . beloved husband of Jennifer and loving father of
Edward Stephen Smith, Claudia Jean (Smith) Robertson,
and bonusson Patrick."

Even if there is animosity between biological and bonuschildren,
I doubt that the biological children would begrudge *any* mention of
your son. That would indeed be very poor ex-etiquette. But if they do,
and your son feels strongly about a mention in the paper, as a last
resort you may want to publish a sentiment of your own:

" . . . beloved husband of Jennifer and loving bonusdad to
Patrick Wilson."

Gravestone Inscriptions

A gravestone is a permanent memorial to a loved one, so it is important to seriously consider the inscription you choose. Gravestones can
be quite costly and cannot be returned if, after additional scrutiny,
you would like to change the wording.

Remember, although the words you choose are a tribute to the
loved one who has passed, those who remain will view them. So
choosing inscriptions for your spouse's gravestone like "one and only
love" or "soul mate and lover" could give a potential future spouse
reason for pause. Even though you know that the love you feel for
your spouse is special and true, phrases like "beloved husband" or
"devoted partner" may prove to be more fitting in the long run.

If the deceased was married at the time of death, it is common to
refer to that relationship on the gravestone: "beloved husband" or
"beloved wife." But if the deceased was divorced at the time of death,
the relationship to the ex is not mentioned. In those cases, just
"devoted father," for example, is appropriate. If the deceased was liv-

ing with someone, then reference to a "longtime partner" can also be appropriate.

Inheritance Issues

After divorce and remarriage and years of compromise and "putting the children first," everyone may get along fabulously until someone passes away, and then there is talk of wills and trusts. Families are more complicated now, and sorting out who gets what after death is far more complex.

For example, a widow whose husband left his estate to his adult children from his first marriage may feel abandoned and neglected and may have to change her lifestyle dramatically. A mother who leaves her estate to her new husband may create a situation in which her adult children feel this newcomer has robbed them of what is rightfully theirs. Biological siblings may unite against their half siblings because they disagree about the distribution of family heirlooms once their parents pass.

You can head off these kinds of scenarios by anticipating problems well in advance and working with your family to improve communication, to problem-solve creatively, and to establish trust while you are together. Arguments begin when family members question the deceased's wishes. With this in mind, be up front with your family about your intentions after your death. Seek good legal advice and responsible financial planning assistance so that questions and uncertainty can be kept at a minimum.

Home Inheritance

"I've been living with a man for two years. We were planning to marry, but he's ill now. If he dies, his kids will want me out of their family house. I'm a senior, age sixty-nine. What are my rights?"

Although you should always check with an attorney who knows your individual case, it is my understanding that you would have no formal rights without marriage or without the home being explicitly bequeathed to you in a will or trust. The standard eviction laws would apply. After the death of a parent, adult children sometimes have a hard time accepting the late parent's new partner. They may see the new person as an interloper and are just not sensitive to his or her plight. Meanwhile, you are an older person who has found love and affection with someone in your golden years but now may be forced to mourn his passing while also looking for a new place to live.

To eliminate these problems, some seniors sell the family home and then purchase a house together with their new partner, with the understanding that if one passes, the other may remain in the home until death. Then the home may be left to both of the seniors' children and either sold or some other agreement made.

It may be the case that your partner has some concern about leaving you the family home, and that may be why he is dragging his feet about marriage. He may want to leave the family home to his children and is simply too embarrassed to tell you. If that is the case, and your real concern is just having a place to live, not inheriting the family home, that information is important for everyone to know. It will eliminate any worry your partner might have about hurting your feelings and will ease his children's minds, too.

I hope that you will all choose to discuss this situation before you're faced with making a decision while grieving the passing of your loved one. Emotions run high at those times, and it would be better if you can make your decisions now, when your reason isn't colored by your grief. Be honest with each other, and let the mutual love you all have for this man guide you in choosing your words.

Divvying Up Family Heirlooms

This is perhaps one of the all-time sore subjects associated with divorce and remarriage—passing on the family heirlooms when the deceased has remarried. Divorced parents, divorced grandparents, and other divorced relatives can do their families a real service by having a will or trust in place before they pass. It may not eliminate bad feelings completely, but it will let it be known in no uncertain terms what you intended. If there is no will, a letter listing who should inherit the furniture or special family possessions, although not legally binding, will give those who remain some direction as to distribution.

If there is no will or trust, and the deceased lives in a "community property" state, all the deceased's property automatically goes to the spouse. When the spouse dies, the possessions go to his or her closest relative. This law, although quite logical, may prevent the biological children from inheriting any of their deceased father's property. For example, if their father has remarried and has no will, after his death his belongings pass to his wife, who may not be the biological mother of his children. When she passes, with no will again, the belongings then go to her nearest relative, most likely her children. They may or may not be related to the man whose passing began this sequence. A will or trust would eliminate the problem.

My mother wore a sizable diamond wedding ring, and the family joke was that the ring was the only heirloom I wanted, and my sister could have all the other jewelry. Good thing I was serious, because that is exactly how my mom spelled out everything in her trust.

I have already told my children to whom I would like to leave various pieces of jewelry and other favorite things when I pass on. My biological daughter from my first marriage gets my mother's wedding ring. She was her oldest biological granddaughter, and I am sure that my mother would have wanted me to pass it on to her. My mother also gave me another ring before her death, and I would like my bonusdaughter to have that ring. My husband and I also have a daughter together, and I have designated the wedding ring that her father gave me to be left to her. My bonusson gets my husband's Harley.

Sharyl and I receive so many queries about the proper way to divvy up family heirlooms after a family member passes. Search your heart for the best solution if the deceased did not leave a clue as to how he or she would have liked things distributed. Don't let greed be your guide. From your past interaction with family members, you know how things should be. Ex-etiquette rule number eight is "Be honest and straightforward." Enough said.

Resources

Organizations

Bonus Families
P.O. Box 1926
Discovery Bay, CA 94514
www.bonusfamilies.com

A nonprofit organization dedicated to peaceful coexistence between divorced or never-been-married parents and their new families. Extensive Web site contains helpful articles and information on support groups and both face-to-face and online mediation.

Parents Without Partners
1650 South Dixie Highway, Suite 510
Boca Raton, FL 33432
www.parentswithoutpartners.org

An international nonprofit educational organization devoted to the interests of single parents and their children.

Books

Books on Divorce and Stepfamilies for Adults

Blackstone-Ford, Jann, and Sharyl Jupe. *Ex-Etiquette for Parents: Good Behavior After a Divorce or Separation.* Chicago: Chicago Review Press, 2004.

Blackstone-Ford, Jann, and Sharyl Jupe. *Ex-Etiquette for Weddings: The Blended Families' Guide to Tying the Knot.* Chicago: Chicago Review Press, 2007.

Block, Joel D., and Susan S. Bartell. *Mommy or Daddy: Whose Side Am I On?* Avon, MA: Adams Media, 2002.

Burt, Anne, editor. *My Father Married Your Mother: Writers Talk About Stepparents, Stepchildren, and Everyone in Between.* New York: W. W. Norton, 2006.

Cohn, Lisa, and William Merkel. *One Family, Two Family, New Family: Stories and Advice for Stepfamilies.* Ashland, OR: RiverWood Books, 2004.

Emery, Robert E. *The Truth About Children and Divorce: Dealing with the Emotions So You and Your Children Can Thrive.* New York: Viking, 2004.

Neuman, M. Gary, and Patricia Romanowski. *Helping Your Kids Cope with Divorce the Sandcastles Way.* New York: Times Books, 1998.

O'Connor, Anne. *The Truth About Stepfamilies: Real American Stepfamilies Speak Out About What Works and What Doesn't When It Comes to Creating a Family Together.* New York: Marlowe, 2003.

Ricci, Isolina. *Mom's House, Dad's House: A Complete Guide for Parents Who Are Separated, Divorced, or Remarried.* New York: Fireside Press, 1997.

Warshak, Richard Ades. *Divorce Poison: Protecting the Parent-Child Bond from a Vindictive Ex.* New York: Regan Books, 2001.

Wisdom, Susan, and Jennifer Green. *Stepcoupling: Creating and Sustaining a Strong Marriage in Today's Blended Family*. New York: Three Rivers Press, 2002.

Books on Divorce and Stepfamilies for Kids and Teens

Block, Joel D., and Susan S. Bartell. *Stepliving for Teens: Getting Along with Stepparents, Parents, and Siblings*. New York: Price Stern Sloan, 2001.

Brown, Laurene Krasny, and Marc Brown. *Dinosaurs Divorce: A Guide for Changing Families*. Boston: Joy Street Books, 1986.

Ford, Melanie, Annie Ford, Steven Ford, and Jann Blackstone-Ford. *My Parents Are Divorced Too: A Book for Kids by Kids*. 2nd ed. Washington, DC: Magination Press, 2006.

Ransom, Jeanie Franz, and Kathryn Kunz Finney. *I Don't Want to Talk About It*. Washington, DC: Magination Press, 2000.

Ricci, Isolina. *Mom's House, Dad's House for Kids: Feeling at Home in One Home or Two*. New York: Fireside Press, 2006.

Web Sites

Divorce Step

www.divorcestep.com

Provides consultation and direct services in the areas of divorce and stepfamily relationships.

Ex-Etiquette

www.bonusfamilies.com/ex-etiquette.php

Help from Jann Blackstone-Ford, M.A., and Sharyl Jupe on interacting with an ex.

Family Medallion

www.familymedallion.com

Jewelry and keepsakes designed specifically for the second marriage.

Second Wives Café

www.secondwivescafe.com

Articles, message boards, and other online resources for second wives and stepmothers.

The Second Wives Club

www.secondwivesclub.com

Online community serving stepmoms and second wives since 1997.

Smart Marriages

www.smartmarriages.com

"The Coalition for Marriage, Family and Couples Education."

STEP-Carefully!

http://stepcarefully.com

A Christian site that offers private stepfamily coaching, family mediation, workshop seminars, support groups, and other stepparenting resources.

Stepfamily Information

www.stepfamilyinfo.org

Nonprofit divorce, remarriage, and co-parenting help.

Stepfamily Network

www.stepfamily.net

The Stepfamily Network is a nonprofit organization dedicated to helping stepfamily members achieve harmony and mutual respect in their family lives through education and support.

Stepfamily Talk Radio

www.stepfamilytalkradio.com

Innovative radio programming for parents who are divorced, separated, remarried, or plan to combine families.

Wives of Widowers

www.wivesofwidowers.com

Online support for wives and soon-to-be wives of widowers.

Index

Also available from Chicago Review Press

304 pages, 6 x 9
Paper, $14.95 (CAN $22.95)
ISBN-13: 978-1-55652-551-3
ISBN-10: 1-55652-551-6

Ex-Etiquette for Parents
Good Behavior After a Divorce or Separation

Jann Blackstone-Ford and Sharyl Jupe

"A remarkable tool for all parents who are separated, divorced or remarried. . . . Jann and
Sharyl are not only experts in the field of
divorce and remarriage, they are also living
proof that it is possible to have a positive relationship with an ex-spouse that will allow you
to continue to raise your children in a harmo-
nious family."

—Dr. Susan S. Bartell, author,
Stepliving for Teens and *Mommy
or Daddy: Whose Side Am I On?*

"Highly recommended." —*Library Journal*

224 pages, 6 x 9
Paper, $14.95 (CAN $18.95)
ISBN-13: 978-1-55652-671-8
ISBN-10: 1-55652-551-6

Ex-Etiquette for Weddings
The Blended Families' Guide to Tying the Knot

Jann Blackstone-Ford and Sharyl Jupe

Weddings rarely go off without a hitch, and
when ex-spouses, children from previous mar-
riages, and multiple sets of in-laws are involved,
couples definitely need brand-new guidelines to
politely maneuver their nuptial plans. Whether
you are remarrying and attempting to combine
two families or a first-time bride or groom dealing with feuding divorced parents, *Ex-Etiquette
for Weddings* helps you navigate a host of emotionally charged situations.